In this important work, John Holm _____
'perennial philosophy' as a gnostic p_____ _____ goal is the highest
transformation of human awareness. Looking not to the past but to
the future, the author instills an esoteric urgency into the task of
self-knowledge that points beyond conceptual thought through
initiatic insights. The new maps of this territory are
multidimensional and theosophical but cannot be constrained to
singular images or designs. What the author offers is an illuminative
journey, a genuine exploration of the territory, in a provocation of
insights that leads beyond all maps into a deepening view of the
experiential Real. This is a work that deserves careful study,
reflection, and appreciation for an esoteric topography that is only
now emerging into articulate human awareness.

Dr Lee Irwin
Chair of the Religious Studies Department at the
College of Charleston

Essential reading for anyone, scholar or seeker alike, who wishes to
understand the roots of the new religiosity that is trying to be born
in our spiritually hungry world.

Jacob Needleman PhD, Professor of Philosophy
San Francisco State University, author of the best-selling
The American Soul and *Why Can't We Be Good*

This is the kind of thorough overview of the perennial wisdom
underlying creation we have needed for a long time. Wise and
thoughtful, it should be on the shelves of everyone concerned with
the spiritual values of our own time and the way these have been
shaped by the past. An important book.

John Matthews, co-author of *Walkers Between The Worlds:*
The Western Tradition from Shaman to Magus

This book is like a strong current that runs beneath the choppy, surface waves of the ocean and controls climates. For those who want - no crave - from their reading something more nourishing, satisfying, and sustaining than the morning's newspaper, on the one hand, and fiction that can while away evenings on the other, this is your book.

Profundity is opposite of superficiality, and this is a profound book. In a way that comes close to being magisterial, Holman weaves the esoteric strands of Western civilization into a tapestry that 'for those who have eyes to see,' is truly beautiful.

It is an important and much needed achievement.

Huston Smith PhD
author of *The World's Religions*

John Holman PhD is an independent scholar who holds degrees in the arts, philosophy and religious studies. Specializing in Western esotericism, he is a leading authority on Hermetic psychology, and a member of the Association for the Study of Esotericism, the Association for Transpersonal Psychology, and the Scientific and Medical Network

Dedicated to my wife,
Tamasine Holman,
for her endless support,
and to my mentor,
Dr Norman Pearson,
for being precisely that.

With thanks also to
Robert Ellwood for his advice
and comments.

The Return of the
Perennial
Philosophy

The Supreme Vision of
Western Esotericism

JOHN HOLMAN

WATKINS PUBLISHING
LONDON

Distributed in the USA and Canada by Sterling Publishing Co., Inc.
387 Park Avenue South, New York, NY 10016

This edition first published in the UK and USA 2008 by
Watkins Publishing, Sixth Floor, Castle House,
75–76 Wells Street, London W1T 3QH

1 3 5 7 9 10 8 6 4 2

Designed and typeset by Jerry Goldie

Printed and bound in Great Britain

Library of Congress Cataloging-in-Publication Data Available

ISBN 13: 978-1-905857-58-6
ISBN 10: 1-905857-58-6

www.watkinspublishing.co.uk

For information about custom editions, special sales, premium and
corporate purchases, please contact Sterling Special Sales
Department at 800-805-5489 or specialsales@sterlingpub.com.

Contents

List of Figures

True it is; know with sure admiration

That the high is the same thing as the low

From all to one through one to all must go

All wondrous effects of adaptation.

One is nursed to all through meditation,

As nurse and womb and parents it shall know

Earth, the wind, Diana and Apollo

In this thing alone lies all perfection.

Changed into earth its power is entire:

Gently separate the earth from the fire.

The subtle with great wisdom from the coarse.

From the earth it climbs to Heaven then to aspire

To earth once more where it will gain the force

Of each the high and low that all require.

The Emerald Tablet

Foreword

The Western Esoteric Tradition is increasingly emerging into view. It has always been there, but has often been hidden, *occult*, or enclosed, *esoteric*. One could call it the Western Alternative Reality Tradition, or better, as John Holman together with others has labelled it, the Perennial Philosophy, that wisdom which like the tide may rise and fall, but does not die. Alongside the exoteric spiritual preachments of Judaism and Christianity, with their emphasis on faith, devotion, and exemplary moral practice, another voice has said: 'Yes, those are important, but there is still more. Behind, beside, within, hidden, lies a pearl of great price, toward which the columns of outer creeds are but pointers: call it mysticism, for it is best realized through states of mind that transcend ordinary reason or "linear" thinking; call it wisdom in the sense of *gnosis*, not plain knowledge alone, but insight based on experience as to the nature of ultimate reality and our place in it; call it initiatory, for this gnosis is best attained through a series of inward awakenings or rebirthings, like transiting from the world of dreams to the light of day, or passing anew from the darkness and security of the womb to the realm of sky and sun.'

An initiation is above all the ordeal, leading into wonder, of Plato's escapee from the cave, from flames and reflections into the light, where the dazed wanderer from a realm of shadows sees the sun for the first time in all its blinding brilliance; but who, on returning to the dungeon of his erstwhile fellow-captives, will be mocked more than believed. The Western alternative tradition has roots in ancient Platonism, and even that which lies behind the Greek philosopher's images: Pythagoreanism, Eleusis, the Mysteries, perhaps primordial shamanism. From Plato it may be traced through Neoplatonism, Gnosticism, the Kabbalah, Alchemy, the Renaissance occult revival, Rosicrucianism, the various Freemasonic and kindred lodges of the eighteenth century and after, and in nineteenth century movements like Theosophy and the Hermetic Order of the Golden Dawn. In the twentieth and twenty-first centuries the legacy of the mysteries can be traced in numerous teachings, and in the mystique of the 1960s counterculture and what is called the New Age movement. All these, under many names and symbols, lead us to believe that profounder levels of understanding, of ourselves and our universe, can be known than just the ordinary or even the 'scientific', and they have mounted initiatory scenarios to assist us in that journey. In the early twenty-first century, as a recent spate of conferences and books (e.g. the works of recognized scholars like Antoine Faivre, Joscelyn Godwin, and Huston Smith) makes evident, a revival of interest on both academic and popular levels in this tradition is taking place. No longer dismissed as fringe or irrational, it is accepted as having a table in the marketplace of ideas, presenting serious offerings both philosophically and experientially.

John Holman, in *The Return of the Perennial Philosophy*, contributes significantly to this revival. Focusing particularly on the initiatory path, but also bringing out convergences of the esoteric tradition with the psychologies of major figures like C. G. Jung and Roberto Assagioli, he makes clear that, on deep levels, the esoteric tradition and the perennial philosophy speak to contemporary yearnings and uncertainties, as well as filling in blanks in the Western history of ideas.

To be sure, in the last few centuries especially (and this may also have been the case in antiquity), Eastern and Western initiations and perennial philosophies have mingled. Of course salient parallels may be obtained between, say, initiation in Sufi or Tantric orders and those of Western lodges, and the timeless wisdom of the Absolute is ultimately one, whether Vedanta, Buddhist, or Neoplatonic. Yet Holman is right here to focus on the Western tradition. Ironically, it is less well known to many Western seekers than the Eastern tradition, but possessing its own richness and beauty, it deserves to be lifted out and presented by itself and for its own sake. This volume will be a valuable part of that presentation, and it is recommended to all who wish to know more about a heritage both known and unknown.

Robert Ellwood, PhD
Distinguished Emeritus Professor of Religion
University of Southern California

Author's Note
The path of the perennial philosophy has been and continues to be trodden by both men and women. For readability, the male pronoun is used throughout this text. It should nonetheless be read as referring to both sexes.

Introduction

AIMS AND STRUCTURE

The principle aim of this book is to paint a picture of the Western esoteric worldview – a picture that might discursively function as the perennial philosophy according to esotericism. The focus will be on the psychospiritual and cosmological aspects (the social, political, and cultural aspects being reserved for a later work), and, whilst the author holds his hands up to the charge of syncretism, it is hoped that this picture would be one that is largely recognized by *practitioners*. A secondary aim is the illumination of modern theosophical teachings particularly concerning *initiatology* – a subject which, to date, has been little understood or at least explored in depth. It is hoped that this exposition in particular will serve to stimulate fresh debate between thinkers in the fields of religion, psychology, and mysticism.

The next section of this introduction will consider the thorny issue of methodology in the study of esotericism. Part One of the book will consider the principles of the 'Ageless Wisdom' as formulated by, first, the early esotericists, associated with the schools of Gnosticism, Neoplatonism and Hermeticism.[1] This will be followed by a consideration of Traditionalism – the school associated chiefly with the names of René Guénon, Ananda Coomaraswamy, and

Frithjof Schuon; and then the Theosophy of H P Blavatsky and her successors, including Rudolf Steiner and Alice Bailey, who professed to give us a fuller and deeper esoteric teaching for the present age. The last chapter of Part One will consider some other esoteric schools; namely, Christian Theosophy, Kabbalism, and Alchemy.

The reader should understand that the author's intention was not to provide an encyclopaedia of esoteric schools and their ideas,[2] but rather to build up layers of a generic and, hopefully, comprehensible picture. The consideration of the essential teachings of *these* schools, in the order that they are, was identified as a means for providing this. The result can be seen as both a new interpretation of existing schemata, and a new synthetic offering – a single and coherent esoteric philosophy, which has a distinctly arithmosophical character, and which features a uniquely vital theogony. The new interpretation might serve as the basis for a new field of comparative esotericism (see Figure 7), and the new offering has as its backdrop a 'standard perennial philosophy map' that has its metaphysical shortcomings (see Chapter 13).

Part Two of the book will consider in some detail the spiritual or initiatory path leading, as we shall see, to a destination at once familiar and surprising. The spiritual path in esotericism is not merely the science of self-realization; it has a larger cosmic and teleological context. This context will be identified, and the relationship between common cross-cultural mystical experiences (such as the 'pure consciousness event' and the 'dark night of the soul') and occult initiations will be discussed. Part Three of the book will consider the subject of changing worldviews from the modern to the postmodern and beyond; also, the train of psychospiritual thought (passing through Carl Jung, Roberto Assagioli, and Ken Wilber) that has, more than anything else perhaps, served to put the idea of the perennial philosophy back in discussion. The final chapter of the book will conclude in the form of 'challenges' of the esoteric view – challenges, that is, to both the worldview of secular humanism and classical physics, *and* some contemporary holistic or 'new age' views.

Historical Introduction

The coining of the term *philosophia perennis* is generally attributed to Gottfried Wilhelm Leibniz (1646-1716), who used the term to signify what was needed to complete his own system. This was to be, says W T S Thackara, an eclectic analysis of the truth and falsehood of all philosophies, ancient and modern, by which (quoting Leibniz) 'one would draw the gold from the dross, the diamond from its mine, the light from the shadows.'[3] The perennial philosophy would thus be the fruit of a particular analytical project, and views among philosophers since Leibniz have differed as to whether such a 'final' philosophy was earlier achieved or is achievable, and whether the idea is simply the idea of philosophy itself. Certainly we can speak of the perenniality of philosophy and the universality of certain questions and concerns.

Leibniz himself did not claim to invent the term: he drew it from an earlier work – *De Perenni Philosophia* (1540) by the theologian Agostino Steuco (1497-1548). The object for Steuco was an originally revealed absolute truth – a *prisca theologia* by another name. For Frances Yates, an important earlier scholar of esotericism, the *prisca theologia* was the 'pristine fount of illumination flowing from the Divine *Mens*'.[4] The concept of a perennial philosophy as the first (and presumably also the last, because it is absolute) wisdom is of great antiquity. Thackara gives as an example the Roman statesman Marcus Tullius Cicero (106-43 BCE), who referred to an original and universal Wisdom-religion. An absolute wisdom would be such because it is God's wisdom – *Theo-sophia* – and this term has been used most of all by esoteric writers from Ammonius Saccas in the 3rd century through to Helena Blavatsky at the end of the 19th century and on to today.

Aldous Huxley: The Perennial Philosophy

Aldous Huxley's *The Perennial Philosophy* (1944) presents itself as an anthology of the perennial philosophy – its principles and themes – and in it the author argues that the ideal society depends upon the dissemination and general acceptance of a form of the perennial philosophy. By 'a form of' he refers to a distinction between the perennial philosophy *itself* as Divine Reality, and metaphysical schemes that are attempts to formulate such. Divine Reality cannot be directly and immediately apprehended 'except by those who have chosen to fulfil certain conditions', he says, and 'to few professional philosophers … is there any evidence that they did very much in the way of fulfilling the necessary conditions.'[5] We have only second-hand accounts or conceptions of Divine Reality then, but these furnish us with material for reflection, and furthermore we can go beyond these to the Truth itself, if we submit ourselves to the same spiritual discipline as those who have 'trod the Path' before us.

Huxley's themes include charity, the real meaning of which is divine love (which itself is unconditional), not simply almsgiving or kindness; the value of rites and symbols – important as pointers, but the distinction between rite/symbol and reality must be clearly recognized; and time and timelessness – we are to understand that the ground of all existence is 'not merely a continuum, it is also out of time'.[6] The principles of the perennial philosophy he articulates (drawing upon traditional Eastern and Western religious sources), include: 1) the immanence and transcendence of God as a 'Pure Consciousness' that lives the human self as an actor lives his part, making the manifold world of our everyday experience 'real with a relative reality … but this relative reality has its being within and because of the absolute Reality';[7] 2) the principle that the work to be achieved by human beings is union in consciousness with God – this requires us in some measure to 'die to self' in order to 'make room' for God;[8] and 3) the principle that in no period has God or Divine Reality left Himself (or Itself) without representation, through prophets/mystics and their teachings.

THE STUDY OF WESTERN ESOTERICISM
The Field Today

Western Esotericism is a relatively new academic field and, as such, there is not yet agreement on what is included and excluded from study. 'Western' is an issue, where there is or might be an esoteric

Buddhism, an esoteric Taoism etc.; so too is a field of esotericism distinct from the more established one of mysticism. Then there is the overshadowing problem – not confined to the subject of esotericism (as just one subject under the rubric of the study of religion) – of the meta-empirical. The Greek *esoterikos* is formed on *eso* meaning 'inner', and the suffix *-ism* can denote a system, principle, or ideological movement (as in Marxism), or an action or its result (as in baptism). Presently, the esotericism studied is an historical thought-train; what we might call the 'underground' tradition of Western thought, connected with such schools as those considered in Part One.

The concern here, says Wouter J Hanegraaff, is to shed light on such 'specific interrelated historical currents in [particularly] modern and contemporary Western culture, which have largely been neglected or disregarded by earlier generations'. The purpose of this pursuit is to fill in 'serious gaps in our knowledge, with predictably negative effects upon the understanding of our own cultural heritage'.[9] Other scholars in the field include Antoine Faivre, Jean-Pierre Brach, Nicholas Goodrick-Clarke, Arthur Versluis, Joscelyn Godwin and Kocku von Stuckrad. The approach commonly promoted (if not prescribed) is the 'agnostic-empirical'. What is observable to all of us (with some effort, and with the ordinary human mind) is the *conceptions* of the esotericists – not what these conceptions are or may be *of* (Divine Reality). These conceptions, as we elicit them, are to be presented 'neutrally' (i.e. without expressing an opinion on their veracity), and this student of Western Esotericism is, to be clear, *operationally* not an esotericist but, as Faivre proposes to differentiate, an 'esoterologist'.[10]

One problem with this approach is this: take, for example, Rudolf Steiner's book *Occult Science: An Outline* (1910). One may dissect this book for its conceptual make-up, and report these as one's findings, but these findings would not be those of *Steiner's* study. Versluis, accordingly, proposes a different approach, which he calls the 'sympathetic empirical'. If we want to accurately and adequately convey an esotericist's view, then we have no alternative but to some degree to walk in his or her mental shoes. 'It is essential for scholars to engage at minimum in a process of imaginative participation', he says. 'Yet I will go further ... I am suggesting that in order to fully understand what we are studying, there is a point in this field ... at which the practitioner's expertise takes on more importance than purely academic knowledge.'[11]

The practitioner here is the esotericist – he or she whose expertise comes from treading the Path, with all that this entails, including a desire for spiritual rebirth in the first place. Versluis is a particular authority on Christian Theosophy (the school associated chiefly with the name of Jacob Boehme), and Boehme wrote: 'None should think or desire to find the lily of the heavenly bud with deep searching and studying, if he not be entered by earnest repentance in the New Birth, so that it be grown in himself.'[12] The scholar's own central motivation will ultimately determine the how and what of approach. As thinkers influenced by the postmodern Zeitgeist, we might automatically reject the idea of an ultimate philosophy, and impress this 'correct under-standing' onto our students. But Jacob Needleman for one insists on the esotericism that is the 'movement within oneself toward inner freedom or, to use another language, toward God'.[13] Hanegraaff believes that there is 'ample room for various approaches to complement each other as well as compete with each other in a con-structive manner, within a general context of methodological pluralism'.[14] Whether this can include the approach of the practi-tioner is, of course, the big question.

An 'Ethnomethodological' or Gnostic Approach

'An empirical or a phenomenological approach to the "alternative real-ity tradition", however much it may reveal about its locations and influences in the world of thought, cannot of itself lead to any true understanding of its essential content', says William Quinn.[15] If we want to truly understand esotericism, the only approach is that of an 'insider'. After all, 'it is both a semantic and metaphysical inversion to attempt a phenomenology of noumena.'[16] 'The time for the kind of rational-ist cataloguing of "superstitious errors of the past" ... is long past', says (perhaps hopes) Versluis, 'but other dangers still remain, ranging from gullible naiveté on the one extreme, and hyperintellectual objectification on the other.'[17] The field seeks to establish itself within the academic mainstream, but the nature of the field itself asks serious questions of the scholar's motivation and, in the end, his *allegiance* (to the academic community with its goal of objective knowledge, or to the wider community of life with its goal of self-realization). Time will tell whether we can have conferences attended by, and presentations given by, esoterologists and esotericists alike. Similarly, for the acceptance that the instantly labelled 'religionist' might not simply be a believer, but someone who knows Divine Reality through his or her practice.

The empirical-historical approach is undoubtedly valuable in filling in gaps in our intellectual heritage, and many esotericists themselves have been historians, or at least incorporated a lot of historical research into their work (G R S Mead and Manly P Hall for instance). But where the historical record is capitalized, there is the danger of losing sight of the essentials and/or failing to effectively communicate them. The reader, as 'diner', receives his 'starter' (the history of the esoteric school), and 'pudding' (the historical influence of that school's teachings in the world of ideas), but needs to go elsewhere for his 'main course' (the profound content of the esoteric teachings). Some scholars appear content to paint the view of just one esotericist or school, whilst others busy themselves with defining the boundaries of the academic field and/or establishing esotericism in the history of ideas.[18] Perhaps it is left to an author with a somewhat non-traditional background to attempt to paint a picture of esotericism as a whole.

> Those that hold public Honours and Offices or be always
> busied with private and necessary occupations, let them
> not strive to attain unto the acme of this Philosophy; for it
> requireth the whole man, and being found, it possesseth
> him, and he being possessed, it debarreth him from all
> other long and serious employments, for he will esteem
> other things as strange, and of no value unto him.
>
> Jean d'Espagnet [19]

Overstating the point perhaps, but it is true one must be 'full-time' on the Great Work, with theurgic practice coming before scholarly activity. We can be esotericists as well as esoterologists but, crucially, we need not be esoterologists to be esotericists. Moreover, the practice of esoterology, though it may awaken in us the need to 'walk the walk' and not just 'talk the talk', is utterly different to the practice of esotericism. After all, we can gain a PhD in sports science without being athletes ourselves. We can know all the theories on, and conceptualizations of, and have read all the descriptions by athletes of 'the zone', without having had the personal experience of the same. It is only by having personal experience of the same that we can truly know *that*, and *what*, such is.

If the findings of practice A (esoterology) are that there is no perennial philosophy, it is because this practice is dealing with ideas, and not what we might call 'metrics of being'. This is what practice B (esotericism) deals with. The academic world is divided into disciplines, as the geopolitical world is divided into nations, and there needs to be a transdisciplinary approach to epistemological problems, as there needs to be a transnational approach to global problems. But infected with the postmodern virus (see Chapter 10), we find it easy to be 'inter-' and 'multi-', but hard to be 'trans-'. Our illness *is* the conviction that the deepest level of man and truth is culture and language respectively.

The Procedure and Its Implications

The whole essence of esotericism is 'hidden truths' – truths that are hidden to all except those who follow the necessary 'procedure' to know them and their nature. This procedure involves the study of texts *as a support activity only*, meaning that ordinary scholarly research – however much it may reveal of an empirical domain we call 'Western esoteric thought' – will, by its limited nature (being non-procedural), always remain in orbit of the real material. The 'space station' that is the world of thought on esotericism will forever be a flux of form; the real material, as it is not made of thought-stuff at all, will ever be unchanging, both 'ageless' and 'wisdom'.

As a person follows the procedure, so he becomes an esotericist, and his project to understand esotericism is supported by – nay, truly begun with – experience of the esoteric domain. This experience is of such a kind as to eclipse mere mental mastication. The extent of practitioners' knowledge will depend upon how fully they follow the procedure, and their length of service in doing so. Representations of the Ageless Wisdom in systemic form will therefore be more, or less, adequate and complete – and in any event idiosyncratic, according to the esotericist's background and intellectual equipment. We study the esotericist's life and times as *fundamentally causal* incorrectly.

When a person knows that putting one's hand in a flame hurts (from doing this), he cannot remain 'agnostic' on the matter, and he now carries a *didactic* responsibility. In executing this, he will be to some extent exiling himself from the community he was formerly a member of (in this analogy, small children before they know that putting one's hand in a flame hurts too). It *is* intellectual honesty to admit uncertainty where such exists, but where it does *not*, it would be both dishonest and *harmful* to do so (the world needing to be constantly reminded of the existence of 'the Tradition': this itself having a salvific effect). We therefore find the voice of esotericism to be *diaphanic*, as per David A Dilworth's definition.[20] It is a quantum leap, and one we may not wish to make, but we have to accept that there are not just believers and observers with their 'emic' and 'etic' perspectives respectively. Also, we have to consider the savant's responsibility, considering his status in society as an 'expert', with respect to the message that he conveys. To say that there is no perennial philosophy in thought or language would not be incorrect (or irresponsible). To say that there is no perennial philosophy altogether – that's another matter.

For fellow scholars in the field, the author's proposition is that we resist the hegemony of naturalism and the enticements of poststructuralism, not out of acceptance of a religious belief but out of cognizance of the gnostic practice. We do not assert a perennialist view,[21] but we do affirm the perennial injunction 'man, know thyself.'

We do not turn our classrooms into mystery schools or evangelize, but we do encourage contemplation as well as analysis of esotericism, as it manifests in thought, in literature, and *in ourselves*. For at a time when some scientists think they are close to a complete theory of everything, and the commodification of knowledge (and all else) continues apace, esotericism as a subject is not a religion, nor a mere point of debate, but is itself an admonition – a healthy slap in the face.

PART ONE

THE PERENNIAL PHILOSOPHY

1 Early Esotericism

GNOSTICISM

In the ancient world of the first few centuries CE, centred upon the cosmopolitan city of Alexandria in Egypt, a number of religious sects and movements, some operating within the then nascent Christianity, held as their central view the essence of man as a 'divine spark', or 'dreamer' that needs to be awakened to Divine Reality, through the work of gnosis. This word is often defined as salvific or intuitive knowing, and for these early esotericists, man was regarded as possessing a faculty (only needing to be developed) of higher intellection, through which direct knowledge of Divine Reality could be had. Gnostics were not content to, nor was it the intention that they should, 'know' through other people's gnosis. They were to become initiates into the Mysteries themselves, although at the same time great redeemer-revealer figures were thought to have shown human beings the way. The term 'Gnosticism' was a later invention: the various groups and schools at the time usually took their name from their leaders or founders (e.g. Simon Magus, Bardaisan, Basilides, and Valentinus).

The teachings of these early Gnostics come to us chiefly through the Nag Hammadi Library of Coptic scriptures discovered in 1945, and also through a few earlier discovered codices and the references of the heresiologist Church Fathers. The origin of Gnostic thought is hotly debated: one problem is the similarity with much in earlier Greek thought (chiefly Pythagoreanism and Platonism), the thought of some Jewish mystical sects (e.g. the Essenes), the cult of Serapis and the Mithraic and Eleusian mysteries, the religions of Mandaeanism and Manichaeanism further east (in what is now Iraq and Iran), and Hermeticism (where Hermes is the redeemer-revealer). Hence the continued assertion by some thinkers of an older universal Wisdom-religion. We can certainly speak of a *Christian* Gnosticism where Christ is the redeemer-revealer, although to what extent this was merely an attempt by some Gnostics with a religion 'all their own' to infiltrate and shape Christianity before its orthodox codification, is something we must consider. It is interesting to note, for instance, that in the 2nd century, Valentinus narrowly lost an election to become Bishop of Rome. Also, it wasn't until after the Council of Nicea in 325, that Jesus as the one and only Son of God (rather than simply a master of gnosis) became official Christian doctrine.[1]

FIGURE 1: THE GNOSTIC COSMOS

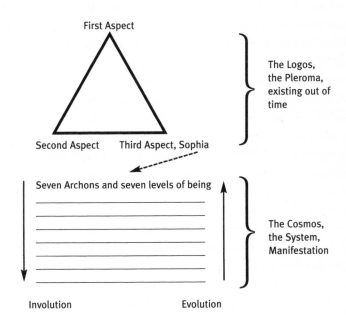

First Aspect

Second Aspect Third Aspect, Sophia

The Logos, the Pleroma, existing out of time

Seven Archons and seven levels of being

The Cosmos, the System, Manifestation

Involution Evolution

A common Gnostic cosmology featured an original and transcendental spiritual unity – as ultimate God, the *Logos*, and as 'fullness', the *Pleroma*. Some Gnostic thinkers (e.g. Simon Magus) emphasized three aspects to this God, giving us a triple Godhead (as in orthodox Christianity), with *Sophia* (Wisdom) occupying the Holy Spirit position. The manifest cosmos (where *cosmos* can perhaps best be defined as 'system') to many Gnostics featured seven levels of being, and in its manifestation was the realm of seven *Archons* (rulers or builders), connected in some way with the seven planets (Saturn, Jupiter, Mars, the Sun, Venus, Mercury, and the Moon). Chief among the Archons, identified with materiality, was the *Demiurge*. Human beings find themselves in the manifest cosmos and contain a spark of God (*pneuma* or spirit) – this is one aspect of ourselves, the other two being our form in the manifestation (*hyle*), and the middle aspect of *psyche* (soul or consciousness).

There is a 'Great Work' to be undertaken by human beings, which is to unite in consciousness with God – the sparks going back to the flame, as it were. Before this, they 'slumber in their material prison, their self-awareness stupefied by forces of materiality and mind', says Stephan Hoeller.[2] In the teaching of Bardaisan, Christ descended through the seven levels into physical incarnation (finding himself in the manifestation, as we do), and then ascended through them (as we are to). We may identify ground for an involutionary-evolutionary perspective here, and present too in Gnosticism is a concept of Sophia (part of a Godhead that is out of time remember) as 'mother principle' to the Archons, making these spiritual powers from a certain angle part of a *redemptive* plan. In the Valentinian system, the manifest cosmos is thus not to be hated and material life renounced (although the face of Gnosticism on the whole displays an aversion to the sensible world) because, as David Brons says, it was all 'part of the process of redemption'.[3]

NEOPLATONISM

Like Gnosticism, Neoplatonism is a modern term. The Neoplatonists called themselves Platonists, or at least saw themselves as carrying on the work of Plato, who was regarded as a member of a long line of Wisdom-teachers that also included Pythagoras, Orpheus, and Zoroaster (to whom the *Chaldean Oracles* is attributed). This Wisdom featured a Deity – the One or Supreme Principle – as the source out of which everything flows, without becoming separated from it and with no compromise to its effulgence. Deity can thus be understood as both transcendent and immanent, as the flow is not a temporal process 'but is timeless history'. Furthermore, many Neoplatonists recognized the One and *Ones* – God and Gods (so perhaps system and systems) – with the Gods being understood by Manly Hall as modes of universal consciousness or 'degrees of awareness in space'.[4]

With this God and Gods view, there was a common sympathy for polytheism in Neoplatonism, and also an eclectic philosophical tendency, with Ammonius Saccas (about whom little is known, but who is often regarded as the first of the Neoplatonists) founding a school with aims similar to those of the modern Theosophical Society. Unlike Gnosticism, the attaining of unitive *knowledge* rather than unitive *being* was emphasized (we might analogize and say that whereas the Gnostic was like a person whose desire is to be a great athlete, the Neoplatonist was like a person whose desire is to know the secrets of success in athletics – although such secrets are not revealed except to one who is *in* athletics i.e. an athlete). There was a true practice of philosophy with this goal, which was a long and difficult training. The fully trained philosopher was thus an initiate into the Mysteries, rather than somebody who is merely trained in analytical reasoning which, says Hall, 'is a separative impulse whose natural trend is to break up similars into dissimilars and thereby unduly emphasise them'.[5]

Divine Intellect (Nous)	–	Divine Thinker	⎫
Discursive reason	–	discursive thinker	⎬ Soul
Lower faculties	–	lower being	⎭

Neoplatonism features a Divine Intellect or *Nous* as the faculty by which we may know the Divine Ideas, which are the laws and formulaic structure of the cosmos (the logoic system we find ourselves in). The Indian sage Patanjali spoke of a 'raincloud of knowable things', which are perhaps the very same Ideas. The Soul in its highest manifestation (referring to the initiate) was the Divine Thinker. In the intellectual but uninitiated man it was the discursive thinker, and the Soul in fact manifested in all being/beings. In Neoplatonism, it was not only human beings that had a Great Work to achieve – in some way, all beings had an ascension or evolution to the One ahead of them, and a will to do this (or a natural 'upwards' urge) built into their natures. Peter Kingsley expresses this Neoplatonic view: 'Every single human being is an unconscious immortal. But this is the least of it ... Immortal life is everywhere ... and aching in the depths of its being to return home.'[6] The true practice of philosophy involved, together with study, moral purification, and mystical practice, and in the last connection, Hall believes the Neoplatonists were familiar with Asiatic forms of meditation.[7] We might wonder if this included the Raja Yoga of Patanjali.

After Saccas, some prominent Neoplatonic thinkers (Neoplatonism was a major thought stream in the first six centuries; the Platonic Academy in Athens closing only in 529) were Plotinus, Iamblichus, Proclus, and Macrobius. Plotinus was a student of Saccas (two others were Porphyry and Origen), and he is known to have attacked those Gnostics who demonized the material world. In Neoplatonism, although the lowest level of reality can be thought of as the darkest (that is, most hiding the divine light), at the same time, as it reveals the Soul, it must yet be good, or at least accepted neither positively or negatively. Iamblichus wrote a treatise on the Mysteries of Egypt, and cautioned against a purely intellectual approach (i.e. one not accompanied by moral purification and mystical practice). In the system of Proclus, we find a dividing of the One into a Three-in-One. And as Antoine Faivre notes, Macrobius taught that the Divine Intellect was common to both human and celestial beings (Gods). [8]

HERMETICISM

Hoeller and Hall both describe Hermeticism as a pagan form of Gnosticism, with the same concepts of a divine trinity and a sevenfold manifestation. In Hermeticism it was Hermes, not Christ, who was the redeemer-revealer, and like the Neoplatonists, the Hermeticists appreciated earthly existence more as a condition of opportunity than of imprisonment. The 'Fall of Man' was a valuable descent allowing for the redemption or glorification of the world through the making of a 'Heaven on Earth'. The major Hermetic writings, the *Corpus Hermeticum*, were written in the second or third centuries.[9] Their legendary author was Hermes, a figure who appears in Greek mythology as the messenger of the gods (carrying the symbolic caduceus staff), whose Roman equivalent was Mercury, and who was also identified with the Egyptian God of Wisdom, Thoth. In the larger esoteric tradition that comes down to us, 'thrice-greatest' Hermes (Hermes Trismegistus) was an ancient philosopher-sage who was the first to proclaim himself 'the light of the world', and who taught how immortality could be achieved through linking human consciousness with the light that was divine consciousness.

Very much a central theme in Hermeticism was the idea of spiritual initiations. If a Gnostic school was more of an ashram, a Hermetic school was more of a secret society – 'a sort of Masonic lodge', says Gilles Quispel[10] – where students were instructed on the way of initiation that led to them joining their ascended brothers in *Superbia* (understood as both a psychic condition and a kind of 'kingdom'). This Way (usually capitalized) was the 'Restoration', and a closer connection appears to have been made in Hermeticism between the individual's Great Work and both its result, and the obligation along the Way, of those graced with success in it – the 'heavenization' of the world. Hermeticism taught of a Great Chain of Being from God to rocks, passing through Gods, angels, sages, men, animals, and plants, with each order 'mentoring' (or meant to) in some manner the order below. In one of the Hermetic texts, *The Key*, Hermes says to his pupil Tat: 'The higher, further, have in charge the lower; the Gods look after men, men after animals irrational, while God hath charge of all.'[11] This hierarchical and

7

'educational' organization of Nature was to be the model for the organization of human society.

The Dot, the Line, and the Circle

In Hermeticism, as in the teachings of many Gnostics and Neoplatonists, there were three types of men: the unawakened or material, the awakening or psychic, and the awakened or spiritual. Hall, who is disinclined to essentially differentiate the three schools, discusses in his book *Lectures on Ancient Philosophy* (1929) the symbols of the dot, the line, and the circle that relate to these three types. The dot represents the spirit or pneuma, and the line the involving-evolving soul or psyche (here the downwards-upwards Gnostic picture is replaced by an outwards-inwards picture). The circle represents the manifest extent of the system. The unawakened identify with the circle, the awakening with the line, and the awakened with the dot. If God is the Pure Consciousness that lives the human spirit as an actor lives his part, as Huxley says, then the unawakened are those whose awareness is that of the characters in the play who don't know they are such; the awakening are those who are waking up to their character-illusion (through sequential initiations); and the awakened are those whose awareness is united with the divine actor or author. With this union, said Plotinus, 'the man is changed, no longer himself nor self-belonging; he is merged with the Supreme, sunken into it, one with it: centre collides with centre.'[12]

FIGURE 2: THE HERMETIC SYSTEM

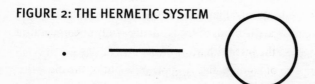

The dot, the centre (out of time); the line, involution; the circle, the extent of the system, manifestation. Then we can picture the circle shrinking back to the dot, with the line this time the Restoration, evolution; and with this the system is redeemed, glorified.

2 Traditionalism

The Western esoteric tradition of theo-sophical currents (or the universal Wisdom-religion in the West, depending on one's perspective), continued chiefly through the Gnostic Bogomils and Cathars from the 10th to the 13th centuries; the mediaeval and Renaissance Alchemists, Hermeticists, and Kabbalists; Rosicrucianism[1] and Christian Theosophy from the 17th century; Martinism[2], Swedenborgianism, and an esoteric Freemasonry from the 18th century; and a Hermetic Occultism associated with the names of Eliphas Lévi, and later Aleister Crowley, Israel Regardie, and Franz Bardon, from the 19th century. With the arrival of Blavatskyan Theosophy at the turn of the 20th century, Buddhist and Hinduist terms entered the Western esoteric vocabulary, and esotericism may be said to have taken (or retaken, thinking of Neoplatonism) a 'comparativist' turn. Western thinkers generally discovered Eastern religions post-Renaissance, and J J Clarke traces this history in his book *Oriental Enlightenment: The Encounter Between Asian and Western Thought* (1997). A key event in this meeting, he says, was the first World's Parliament of Religions in 1893 which, together with providing an opportunity for Eastern religions to speak for themselves (rather than through Western philosophers and theologians), gave impetus to the academic study of comparative religion and, later, the Interfaith Movement.[3]

The discipline of comparative religion grew out of the discipline of comparative philology, says Clarke – the science of religion out of the science of language. We live in a world of many languages and many religions, but could there have been in some distant past, and some equally distant (because gnosis-dependent) present, a single universal Wisdom-religion with its own symbolic language? The idea had not gone away by the end of the 19th century, despite the apparent final 'triumph' of Enlightenment reason over traditional religion and metaphysics with the new positivists, evolutionists, and socialists. For this new generation of material thinkers, says Richard Tarnas, 'this world of man and matter was clearly the one demonstrable reality.'[4] Opposing this view were members of many esoteric groups such as the Hermetic Order of the Golden Dawn, the Martinist Order, and the Gnostic Church, all founded five years before the Parliament (the Theosophical Society was founded in 1875). To these must be added a number of late 19th and early 20th century intellectuals, one of whom was René Guénon (1886-1951) who, as Jean Borella records, was in his earlier life connected with both the Martinist Order and the Gnostic Church.[5]

Attributed by scholars with the founding of the 'Traditionalist' school, Guénon believed in a perennial philosophy (*Sophia Perennis* was his term), as a higher knowledge accessed by the 'intellectual intuition'. This Primordial Wisdom – a term other Traditionalists would use – was not the invention of any particular culture, not was it a recurring set of interdependent metaphysical principles per se. The Truth(s) did, however, find expression through symbols common to the world's major religions, chiefly in their sapiential literature. The individual undertaking the work of gnosis will discover these symbols – what and that they are – in his or her religious tradition, and from this we can speak of an esoteric Christianity, an esoteric Hinduism, etc., but also of esoteric practitioners with a 'religion' all of their own. In the view of Guénon, we may thus arrange in a table of 'knowing' (which may be seen to relate in order to the Neoplatonic Divine Thinker, the discursive thinker with his or her analytical reasoning only, and the Soul manifesting not quite yet as the intellectual but uninitiated man):

1 Esotericists (practitioners)
2 Philosophers, theologians (theorists)
3 Believers

Tradition and Traditional

Scholars speak of a Western esoteric tradition. Guénon simply spoke of 'Tradition'. Something just originating in the past and continuing on would be *a* tradition, but Guénon wished to point our attention to the *Sophia Perennis*/Primordial Wisdom being grounded in the *Aevertinal* (see next section). Most Traditionalists were/are content to speak of *the* Tradition though (the tradition of Tradition if we like), and identify cultures which were, or are, more or less Tradition*al* in their worldview (accepting some 'divine spark' reality at least) and, as a result, their institutions, mores, values, and productions. Some other Traditionalist figures – or names associated with Traditionalism – are Ivan Agueli (1869-1917), Ananda Coomaraswamy (1877-1947), Julius Evola (1898-1974), Henry Corbin (1903-1978), Mircea Eliade (1907-1986), Frithjof Schuon (1907-1998), Titus Burckhardt (1908-1984) and Philip Sherrard (1923-1995). For them all, our modern (post-mediaeval) Western culture is non-Traditional and, we might even recognize, *anti*-Traditional, differing from virtually all other earlier cultures across the globe. Modernity has thus seen a 'degeneration' (as Evola put it) of human civilization into a dark age, where the light of Tradition has been extinguished, or at best glimmers only faintly.

SOME TRADITIONAL PRINCIPLES
Quantity and Quality

The character in the play, man, looks 'horizontally' outwards at an apparent reality of 'this world of man and matter'. This is the quantitative, empirical as opposed to metaphysical dimension. 'Epistemologically, quantity would correlate to discursive ratiocination', says Quinn,[6] and epistemologically, quality would correlate to gnosis – the qualitative dimension is the world of spiritual reality, or what the initiate sees looking 'vertically' inwards. Symbolically, quantity corresponds to the horizontal arm in the two-dimensional cross, and quality to the vertical arm. Sociologically, quantitativization is democratization and the mean average, and qualitativization is the hierarchization of the social order, based upon the locus of the

11

knower (how awakened from the dream they are). The quantitative per se is not the enemy; the enemy is the denial of the qualitative that is so very present in modern Western (which is fast becoming global) thought and culture. We are to individually and culturally rediscover the qualitative dimension and, for Coomaraswamy in particular, the key to this was a Traditional form of education.

The Absolute, the One, Involution and Evolution

If the world is in some sense an illusion, 'fictional', then the God or Logos behind a cosmos-system (Traditionalists, like some Neoplatonists, recognize God and Gods) is what might be called an 'engine of imagination'. Said Hermes to Tat: 'as He [God] thinketh all things manifest, He manifests through all things and in all',[7] and Schuon repeats this idea as a Traditional principle: 'Creation is … something rather like the more or less discontinuous productions of the imagination.'[8] An Absolute behind the One is posited in Traditionalist thought, which pertains to a principle *behind* the logoic nature. The One we are to unite in consciousness with, may be cosmologically *a* One, but to us (as the one in whom *we* live and move and have *our* being) it is *the* One – and, Traditionalists affirm, a threefold One at that. Hence the commonness of the tripartite symbol for God.

We said earlier that for some Gnostics, Sophia was the third aspect of divinity and mother to the Archons. Sherrard does not speak of Archons, but he does talk of a multi-levelled manifestation being continually recreated by the 'immediate activity of spiritual energies'.[9] These energies are inaccessible to the observation of the human reason (as the discursive intellect) and, a fortiori, to that of any instrument devised by it. In Traditionalist writings, we see the idea of the third aspect as the principle of Matter, the second aspect as the principle of Consciousness, and the first aspect as the principle of Spirit. Man has a form in the manifestation and first of all identifies with this. This thing that he identifies with is the principle of Matter become 'actualized' as the relative reality of Matter. He later, as he begins to awaken, identifies with the Hermetic line as opposed to the circle, and this is the principle of Consciousness become actualized too. Finally, he identifies with the Hermetic dot, and this is the actualized first aspect, Spirit. Evolution thus sees a sequence of third aspect-second aspect-first aspect (3-2-1), following an involutionary sequence of 1-2-3.

Aeviternity and Time

God exists out of time and yet through the play which has a time and space all of its own. The events of J R R Tolkien's *The Lord of the Rings* take place over one time (the history that would be measured by a character such as Frodo Baggins in this story), but the time that Tolkien as the engine of imagination behind this fictional world lives in is an altogether different time – an 'esoteric' time relative to Mr Baggins. As Tolkien 'thinketh', all things in Middle Earth manifest, and as the One behind our cosmos-system thinketh, so all things in our sensible reality manifest. Eternity means endless duration and would refer to 'exoteric' time. Aevertinity is the 'always now' (Coomaraswamy called it the 'Nowever'), or the esoteric moment within every moment of exoteric time. The ultimate self of man, the spirit, resides in God, and thus esoteric time. The great mistake of many modern thinkers, says Huston Smith, is to deny the Aevertinal and to introduce development into God, who in ways is made out to be 'not yet'.[10] Schuon agrees: the purely evolutionist view, he says, denies the *constant* 'periphery-centre relationship'.[11]

Three types of time might in fact be acknowledged: 1) the time the character measures; 2) the Aevertinal; and 3) 'Consciousness-time'. One person might take twenty years to achieve union through gnosis, another person ten, another person fifty – consciousness evolution takes place in its own time. Also, as this evolution is a waking up from a dream anyway – taking the man out of a world that doesn't 'really' exist – then Consciousness-time is more fundamental and is the backdrop of 'Character-time'. Aevertinity is more fundamental yet, and is the backdrop of Consciousness-time. Man identifies first with the circle (and Character-time), then with the line (Consciousness-time), and then with the dot (Aevertinity). This means that whilst it may be the year 2008, say, at the same time, it is some point on the return journey (still close to the start perhaps for most people), and at the same time further, we are already (although not yet self-consciously – this being the goal of evolution) living in Aevertinity. The existence of Aevertinity is the reason why Coomaraswamy says (particularly addressing the Eastern thinker) that for the 'central Spectator' (the Spirit) there is no involution/evolution.[12]

Hierarchy and Gnoseology

Reality is tiered: being increases as the levels ascend. This Traditional, Great Chain of Being view, says Smith, though 'commonplace to the point of being universal in the past, is the most difficult for modern consciousness to grasp'.[13] On the tiers are beings *superior* as well as inferior to us, putting us in our true place in the universe. 'Modern science ... can describe our situation physically and approximately, but it can tell us absolutely nothing about our extra-spatial situation in the total and real universe', writes Schuon.[14] Traditionalism recognizes Gods of the type Hall does – degrees of awareness in space – and with respect to these, Smith says: 'We might try to imagine the qualitative difference between the experience of a wood tick and ourselves, and then, continuing in the same expanding direction, introduce orders of magnitude that science has accustomed to us: 10^{23} or whatever.'[15]

Like the Neoplatonists, Traditionalists have a concept of true philosophy, involving more than just study. To think that one can study being (rather than simply philosophies of being) without being transformationally involved in that project is absurd. It is really a case of *avoidance*, says James Cutsinger: 'There is nothing at all new in our wish to avoid the discipline that must accompany all contact with God', for 'the absolute by its very nature requires all that I am. It is satisfied with nothing less than the complete and constant conformity of my entire being.'[16] Traditionalism, like Hermeticism, also recognizes degrees of initiation, and with gnoseology meaning the science of gnosis,[17] we might therefore speak of gnoseology 'undergraduates', 'postgraduates', and 'doctors'. Whilst Schuon and Coomaraswamy were reticent on the idea of a Brotherhood of high initiates/sages in a Superbia (as in Hermeticism), Guénon did speak of an Elect or Elite who were guardians of the Earth's sacred mysteries (recalling the Rosicrucianists' assembly of Adepts), and Evola of a group closely resembling Theosophy's 'Great White Lodge'. We may apparently join this group if we apply ourselves to the same spiritual discipline as they did to join it.

TRADITIONALISM ON HISTORY AND DOCTRINAIRISM

> There is only one mythology, one iconography, and one
> truth, that of an uncreated wisdom that has been handed
> down from time immemorial.
>
> Ananda Coomaraswamy [18]

Theosophy (considered in the next chapter) posits its Lodge going back to the beginning of human history. Their knowledge is of spiritual reality as opposed to the only-apparent reality of the quantitative dimension. The human mind can be turned outwards or inwards, we are told, and whilst history is conceived by Theosophists as the history of the character, man, 'growing into himself' (and thus producing civilizations), this has been 'steered' (or at least tried to be) by the Lodge, whose Wisdom has found expression first in primitive mythologies, then in later mystery religions, and finally in traditional religions and metaphysical philosophies. Traditionalists have a similar understanding – at the very least, with respect to there being a Primordial Wisdom (to access which requires gnosis), and a belief that this can be 'hermeneuticized' out of primitive cultures. Our quantitative dimension-consciousness may have grown over history, says Traditionalism, but until the Middle Ages, the qualitative dimension remained 'acknowledged' in the West through a Great Chain of Being worldview.

Apart from mediaeval Christendom, Guénon highlighted the Vedic Indian and Schuon the Native American (and other Traditionalists the Maori, Chinese, ancient Egyptian, and early Greek) cultures as examples of Traditional cultures. The Theosophist might say that early humanity, before it grew up into the rational adult, was more *impressionable* to the divine teachings. The Traditionalist notes a general decline in our inwards orientation manifesting, among other things, in analytical philosophy replacing true philosophy, the religion of secular humanism replacing traditional religions (themselves losing touch with their esoteric 'heart' through the absence of gnosis), and our ecological irresponsibility through no longer recognizing the brotherhood of Soul(s) as the Neoplatonists did. The modern mentality is no more than the product of a vast collective suggestion, said Guénon, which is that this world of man and matter is the one reality, and for Evola, this turn-about was a 'metaphysical decision' we made (and can therefore unmake) with our free will.[19]

Guénon employed the Vedic classification of ages called the *Krta, Treta, Dvapara*, and *Kali Yugas* to trace our decline. We are in the last of these, where the light of Tradition is most hidden. Many philosophers have presented a 'downwards' order. Allan Combs notes one, the scheme of Giambattista Vico (1668-1744), which features an Age of Gods, an Age of Heroes, and an Age of Men. In the first of these, the gods speak directly to humans through their priests (or their initiatory few, would say the Theosophists and Traditionalists). The last – our own – 'finds government in the hands of ordinary men [not initiates] speaking ordinary language [not the esoteric language]'.[20] In his book *The Reign of Quantity and The Signs of the Times* (1953), Guénon traces the course of Western culture's anti-Traditionalism, beginning with Renaissance humanism and proceeding through Mechanism to Materialism which, he says, 'insinuated itself into the general mentality and finally succeeded in stabilising that attitude, without resort to any kind of theoretical formulation'. Man mechanized everything and finally himself, 'falling little by little into numerical units, parodying unity, yet lost in the uniformity and indistinction of the "mass"'.[21] The darkest age we may be in says

Traditionalism but, as the ages constitute a *cycle*, another Golden Age (in which there would be a dissemination and general acceptance of a form of the perennial philosophy) is inevitably ahead.

Scholars use the word 'Traditionalism' to refer to the thought of Guénon, Schuon, etc. 'Perennialism' may also be used. For Guénon, the word 'traditionalism' 'denotes only a *tendency* which does not imply any *effective knowledge* of traditional truths'.[22] There are real Traditionalists, who are esotericists themselves, whose faculty of knowing is the intellectual intuition; and then there are people whose faculty of knowing is, for now and at best, the discursive intellect. Huxley tells us that the distinction between (esoteric) rite/symbol and reality must be clearly recognized, and only one who is in esotericism (a practitioner) is going to be able to do this.

In his book *The Transcendent Unity of Religions* (1953), Schuon distinguishes between the philosophical, the theological, and the esoteric perspectives. The (analytical) philosopher sees only concepts because his higher faculty not being developed, there is for him no esoteric wisdom and its symbolic representation in metaphysics. The theologian is 'undeveloped' too, but does at least believe in esoteric symbols. Gnostics were not content to know through other people's gnosis, and nor should those be that would be real Traditionalists, is the message. Without 'fulfilling the necessary conditions', those with a tendency towards Tradition will only ever be theorists – and probably doctrinaires – ultimately deferring to the authority of some person such as Guénon or Schuon, or teaching such as theirs.

ADDENDUM: SCHUON ON SYMBOLS, DOGMATISM AND FIRST PRINCIPLES

Today we think of metaphysics as a branch of philosophy, says Schuon, but the truly metaphysical and the esoteric are one and the same. God-consciousness – the Divine Intellect – is in man, and the metaphysical is the content of this. Metaphysical knowledge is therefore purely intellectual (of the Divine Intellect) knowledge – 'pure', because: a) it does not originate from the personal, discursive mind; and b) does not take the form of mutually exclusive ideas, but rather complementary symbols. The idea 'threefoldness' is not the same as the idea 'oneness' – they can't exist in the same philosophical space, as it were. But symbols *can* (and do) exist in the same metaphysical space, as they represent different aspects of the same reality. Schuon uses light to illustrate: Light is light, but the colour white could be said to be its oneness symbol, and the three primary colours together its threefoldness symbol. We have here: a) that which is trans-symbolic; b) complementary symbols; and c) the form those symbols take (colours). For the analytical philosopher, symbols don't exist as a 'higher order' category of representations; he sees only the 'colours'. The theologian doesn't see the symbols as they are either, but he does at least believe they are there. The transcendent unity of religions is not to be found on the levels of faith or of ideas; it is only to be found on the level of metaphysical symbols, for here Buddhist, Christian minds, etc. converge and then dissolve into one transreligious mind.

Dogmatism, says Schuon, doesn't consist in the mere enunciation of an idea, but rather in an interpretation that, 'instead of rejoining the formless and total Truth after taking as its starting point one of the forms of that Truth',[23] attributes to that form an absoluteness that only the formless Truth itself can possess. A dogma is both a limited idea (a discrete form in mind), and an unlimited symbol ('unlimited', because representative of the Divine), at one and the same time – as is man. The exoteric dogma and the exotericist go hand in hand then, as do the esoteric symbol and the esotericist. Schuon gives as an example the dogma of the unicity of the Church. The exotericist says: 'There is but one Church' and has in mind *his* church. The esotericist says the same, but has in mind the esoteric Church, whose members are esotericists. They are united in their essential *divinity* rather than humanity, and this being the case, their Church cannot (and does not) assume any particular human form. A man enters the light through his own religion, but, as this light (the Divine Intellect) is of an order entirely different to the light of his personal, discursive mind, his religion – all religions – are doors to the attic only. Entering the upper part of the living space again (the world of ideas), the man is back with his religion and its dogmas – not that these are dogmas any more, they are symbols. The dogma isn't blameworthy then, only its 'all-invading autocracy' – an autocracy that clamps down (or tries to) as soon as it arises, the esoteric understanding.

Love God with your whole being, said Christ. This obviously includes the philosophical self and, if love is the inclining of one being toward another with a view to union, and the philosophical self is our highest self, then here is the justification for metaphysics/esotericism. The esotericist is he who loves God with his mind – his mind is inclined towards God's mind with a view to union, and this union is the final achievement of his 'love of Sophia'. This union is possible because the Divine Intellect is not someone or something else but himself. The esotericist's journey is not so much driven by a desire for self-deification that could be argued to be an obstacle to salvation, as by a 'logical and ontological tendency toward his own transcendent Essence'.[24] Intelligence does not belong to us – what we regard as our own, is not intelligence in its entirety (it is the personal intellect as opposed to, and which it is dependent for its existence on, the Divine Intellect). For the two to be united, nobleness of soul, piety, and virtue are required. It takes God – it takes *being like* God – to know God: this both the theologian and the analytical philosopher don't fully appreciate, says Schuon. The fideist accepts the reality of inspiration coming from God, but not of an intellectual intuition coming from man, for he is still clinging to the view that there is supernatural revelation, and then there is the (mere) human mind. But man is 'made in the image of God', meaning that man's consciousness is ultimately God's consciousness, and therefore the content of one is ultimately the content of the other.

Elsewhere in *The Transcendent Unity of Religions*, Schuon lists seven core principles which are central to the perennialist thesis: 1) Reality is gradated. It is multi-levelled, with each level of being included in the one above (as the animal consciousness is included in the human consciousness. At the top is Divine consciousness.) 2) Reality is not objective (it is 'God-experience'). 3) God-experience

– the Divine Intellect – is 'behind' the conscious experience of every creature, permitting us to say it is *in* every creature. 4) Beyond God-experience – Being – is Non-Being, the Absolute. 5) The duality of the exotericist is between himself as creature, and God as Being – between two aspects of himself then. The esotericist recognizes the relativeness of this duality. 6) On existence and imperfection: The Absolute is the Ground of Being, constantly 'giving birth' to it. There is no 'Why?' to answer here, for both require the other in order to be what they are (as darkness-light). The latter, Being, is imperfect because otherwise there would be nothing to distinguish it from Non-Being – and then neither would be. 7) On free will: Existence is inescapable, and in this we may say we have no free will. This is only so with respect to our humanity and not our divinity though. To the degree that we divinize ourselves, so our karma will be lifted. The modern worldview is meta-physically barren and thus modern culture reveals an 'intellectuality stripped of intelligence'. By a kind of compensation, says Schuon, 'professional life more and more assumes a "religious" air in the sense that it claims the whole of man, his soul as well as his time, as though the sufficient reason for the human condition were some economic enterprise and not immortality.'[25] Percipient words, perhaps we can agree, for today's world.

3 Theosophy

Guénon saw the Theosophy of Helena Petrovna Blavatsky (1831-1891) as 'pseudo-esotericism', perhaps in espying Theosophical doctrinaires. Quinn remarks that in dismissing Theosophy in toto, was Guénon's 'blind spot', for the similarity in principles in Blavatsky's and Guénon's teachings cannot be denied.[1] We are to be objective, and accept only that which we have discovered for ourselves to be true through gnostic practice. Guénon did teach this, but perhaps sometimes lost sight of his own point in his enthusiasm to steer us towards certain materials for reflection. Blavatsky taught the same point too, her magnum opus *The Secret Doctrine* (1888) being prefaced with the expression 'there is no Religion higher than Truth.' We are to understand this includes the 'religion' of her own Theosophy. Her successor Alice Bailey (1880-1949) was even more explicit, saying: 'The books that I have written are sent out with no claim for their acceptance. They may, or may not, be correct, true and useful. It is for you to ascertain their truth by right practice and by the exercise of the intuition.'[2] Bailey believed that the work of the Lodge had been hindered in modern times by the doctrinairism (if not the dogmatism) of some students or 'disciples' (without naming the culprits). She would have nodded in agreement with Huxley that there are forms of the perennial philosophy, and then there is Divine Reality itself.

Stephan Hoeller regards Theosophy as a continuation of the current of Gnosticism, and Joscelyn Godwin describes Theosophy as 'the most substantial statement of a modern Neognosticism'.[3] Theosophy certainly features the same idea of a triple Godhead or Logos out of time, and a sevenfold manifestation as the realm of seven spiritual powers: this, as the system we find ourselves in. In her earlier life, Blavatsky was connected with Spiritualism and a number of Hermetic-Masonic organizations. In her later life, after travels in the Orient, her work demonstrates a comparativism that Ammonius Saccas perhaps would have been proud of, and her Theosophical Society founded in New York with Henry Steele Olcott (1832-1907) encouraged the study of all religions, philosophies, and science, with members not required (or encouraged) to subscribe to a particular doctrine. In this enlightened attitude lay/lies the 'positive, fruitful contribution' of the Theosophical Society, says Faivre.[4] At the same time, Blavatsky did teach her own scheme, drawing upon Hindu and Buddhist terms, and it is widely acknowledged – as Godwin says – that the Theosophical Society, its members and its offshoots, 'became the main vehicle for Buddhist and Hinduist philosophies to enter the Western consciousness, not merely as an academic study but as something worth embracing'.[5] Theosophy also served to inspire new interest in Buddhism and Hinduism in India, where the international headquarters of the original society remains.[6]

LIFTING THE VEIL: THE ESOTERIC UNIVERSE

We have thoughts about the solar system and the wider universe, wrote G de Purucker, 'but they are not the actual becoming of our consciousness *into* those wider spaces filled with Worlds.'[7] We have been using the analogy of man as a character in a play. Then there is the image of gnosis as a lifting of a veil to reveal an alternate reality – one that is always there, and staring us in the face, but which we are blind to. This is Schuon's total and real universe, featuring Hall's degrees of awareness in space. Theosophy teaches of planetary, solar, and higher consciousnesses (drawing our thoughts back to Smith's 'experiential' orders of magnitude). This is a kind of psychic parallel to the ordinary universe we see of celestial objects of different sizes. These are, furthermore, arranged – or arrangeable – *on different logoic-system levels*. Thus there are beings in one cosmos-system, belonging to a level of such, which have their God. That God is one of a *higher-order* range of beings, in a *higher* cosmos-system, belonging to a *higher* level of such, which have *their* God, and so on. If we live, in some analogous sense, in the 'mind's eye' of an author, then he too – with other authors on his level – lives in the mind's eye of a greater author, and so on.

One logoic-system level:	The range of existence of one group of beings, the lowest level of which constitutes …
A lower logoic-system level:	The range of existence of a lower group of beings, the lowest level of which constitutes …
And so on down	

Theosophists see a universe of degrees of awareness, of consciousnesses – and correspondingly being/beings – 'all the way up'. One degree, which has a primary place in Theosophy, is that belonging to a solar being. Paracelsus wrote of a spiritual sun (perhaps with this being in mind), which 'those whose spiritual senses have awakened to life will see'.[8] His contemporary Heinrich Cornelius Agrippa, author of *De Occulta Philosophia* (1510), also wrote of a spiritual sun to be realized. This no man can do, he says, 'unless he return to the soul of the Sun, and become like to it'.[9] In Theosophy, *our* cosmos-system is the 'body' (actually, the body-*consciousness*) of a solar being. Our God (this solar being) has Himself as a body in His consciousness, just as a man has himself as a body in his consciousness. In a sense, it is *because* of this 'divine' body-consciousness that we *are*. Also, says Theosophy, it is because of a man's body-consciousness that beings on a lower logoic-system level (identified with atoms or cells) are.

'As cells exist in the human body', wrote Manly Hall, 'so man is but a cell in a larger organism which he pleases to term a God'.[10] He might have said: As body-consciousness cells exist in the human body-consciousness, so man (as pneuma, ultimately) is but a body-consciousness cell in a larger body-consciousness (of a solar being). If

Pure Consciousness relates to the consciousness of a 'divine actor', then in Theosophy, Pure Consciousness *for us* relates to the body-consciousness of a solar being. At the end of our evolution, our consciousness 'becomes into' this, but at the same time, it's there all the while in Aevertinity (the difference being, the former is self-conscious achievement). There is *our* solar being/God in Theosophy, *other* solar beings/Gods, and *planetary* beings/Gods – all of these are essentially sited on the next logoic-system level 'up' from ours.

FIGURE 3: THE THEOSOPHICAL HOLARCHY

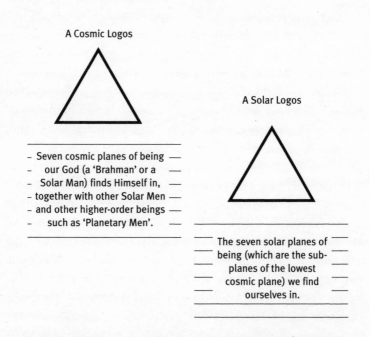

A Cosmic Logos

A Solar Logos

- Seven cosmic planes of being —
- our God (a 'Brahman' or a —
- Solar Man) finds Himself in, —
- together with other Solar Men —
- and other higher-order beings —
- such as 'Planetary Men'. —

The seven solar planes of being (which are the sub-planes of the lowest cosmic plane) we find ourselves in.

'The Solar System is as much the Microcosm of the One Macrocosm as man is the former when compared with his own little Solar Cosmos', wrote Blavatsky.[11] And Bailey wrote: 'The seven planes of the solar system are in the same relation to Him [our God] cosmically as the physical plane is to a human being.'[12] Also, 'the solar Logos is in process of ascertaining His place within the greater system in which He holds a place.'[13]

Our *ultimate* Pure Consciousness as evolutionary goal might then be the body-consciousness of a solar being. But before this there might be a becoming of our consciousness into a planetary being's (i.e. the Earth's) body-consciousness. These solar and planetary Gods on their own logoic-system level still have their God, as said, and therefore both a Pure Consciousness evolutionary goal (and Aevertinal 'pneuma') relating to the body-consciousness of what we might now call a *cosmic* being. On every logoic-system level, writes Brett Mitchell, there is evolution: 'The whole universe is comprised of a hierarchy of Lives, where the smaller evolves into the larger, and the lower consciousness evolves into the higher.'[14] The modern concept of *holarchy* is the idea of a hierarchy of wholes within wholes, or systems complete in themselves yet at the same time part of larger systems. This is the nature of the esoteric universe, affirms Theosophy.

'The existences belonging to every plane of being [on whatever logoic-system level] … are, in degree, of the nature of shadows', wrote Blavatsky, 'but all things are relatively real, for the cogniser is also a reflection, and the things cognised are therefore as real to him as himself.'[15] The ultimate limit of our consciousness 'potential', to repeat the contention, is the lowest level of consciousness of a solar being – our consciousness might then be said to be 'consumed' by that; and the limit of our God's consciousness potential is the lowest level of consciousness of a being Theosophy calls a *Parabrahman*, where our sun is a *Brahman*. (We can say 'a' in both cases, but relative to us this is *the* Brahman and *the* Parabrahman.) Bailey calls our Parabrahman 'The One About Whom Naught Can Be Said' (and might have added 'from where we are in our cosmos-system, on a lower logoic-system level'), and Max Heindel, in his *The Rosicrucian Cosmo-Conception* (1909) calls it 'The Supreme Being', and also the 'Great Architect'.[16] Rather confusingly perhaps, some Theosophists also use the word Parabrahman to refer to an Absolute principle behind any and all logoic systems, as in Traditionalism. Smith notes that in Hindu cosmology there are innumerable tiers vertically,[17] but beyond our Parabrahman, *ontologically and cosmogenetically considered*, Theosophy does not go. Still, here, they would say, is the justification for 'first and last wisdom'.

1st Cosmic Plane

2nd Cosmic Plane

3rd Cosmic Plane

4th Cosmic Plane

5th Cosmic Plane: Relates to a higher order being's e.g. a Solar Man's mental body

6th Cosmic Plane: Relates to a higher order being's e.g. a Solar Man's emotional body

7th Cosmic Plane: Relates to a higher order being's e.g. a Solar Man's physical body

The 7sub-planes of the 7th Cosmic Plane:

1st Solar Plane

2nd Solar Plane

3rd Solar Plane

4th Solar Plane

5th Solar Plane: Relates to a man's mental body

6th Solar Plane: Relates to a man's emotional body

7th Solar Plane: Relates to a man's physical body

Man-the-character thinks, feels and acts. He has a mind, an emotional nature and a body. In Theosophy, he has a mental body, an emotional body and a physical body. Mr Baggins could likewise be seen or said to have a mental, emotional, and physical body, with the mental, emotional, and physical planes of Middle Earth being relatively real. In Hermeticism and Traditionalism, there are several and sequential initiations, and in Theosophy these relate to the planes. Thus *for us*, the first initiation is a seeing-through-the-illusion of a real physical existence (the 7th *solar* plane), and the second initiation is a seeing-through-the-illusion of a real emotional existence (the 6th solar plane). The whole trend traces the character's developing intuition that his existence is fictional; that his essence or true self is to be found, in the Hindu vocabulary, 'beyond *Maya*'. Says Blavatsky: 'The upward progress of the Ego is a series of progressive awakenings ... but only when we shall have reached the absolute Consciousness, and blended our own with it, shall we be free from the delusions produced by Maya.'[18] A Solar Man, apparently, goes through initiations that relate to cosmic as opposed to solar planes.

'IT'S ALL ABOUT CONSCIOUSNESS'

'Consciousness is the one reality, in the fullest sense of that much-used phase; it follows from this that any reality found anywhere is drawn from consciousness', said Annie Besant.[19] Blavatsky too wrote: 'Matter, after all, is nothing more than the sequence of our own states of consciousness, and Spirit an idea of psychic intuition.'[20] For Sri Krishna Prem, 'it should be clear from introspective meditation that all forms are sustained in consciousness', and though scientists commonly think of consciousness as the epiphenomenon of brain activity, the brain itself is one of those forms. 'It is the old story of looking for one's spectacles when they are on your nose ... There is not the slightest reason whatsoever for supposing that anything whatever, physical or mental, exists or can exist save as the content of consciousness.'[21]

Anything whatever includes all concepts (mental forms) of self, matter, reality, etc. It includes therefore all composites of such forms i.e. metaphysical/cosmological schemes. Mr Baggins may take up empirical science and study Middle Earth, but the very existence of his mental body is down to, and is contained within, the conscious-ness of his author. This is why Purucker says that we have thoughts about the solar system and the wider universe, but they are not the actual becoming of our consciousness into those spaces. Bailey's words are interesting in this regard where, in the following quote (written in 1934), the 'Word of Mankind' refers to our Solar Logos, and the 'Word of the Cosmos' refers to Heindel's (and also esoteric Freemasonry's) Great Architect:

One of the great schools of thought or trend of ideas which
is destined to pass away is that of the current philosophies
as we now know them. Philosophy in its technical sense as
the love of wisdom will increase as men understand
increasingly the meaning of wisdom and become epochally
wiser, but the present schools of philosophy have nearly
served their purpose. This has been the formulation of ideas
concerning God and His relation to man, concerning
divinity, eschatology and spiritual relationships. The last
great gestures of the philosophical schools remain yet to be
made. Their place will be taken in later centuries by those
who will in deed and in truth be cosmologists, for once the
Word of Mankind is understood and grasped and the
significance of the individual appreciated, the Word of the
Cosmos will receive due and more correct attention, and
the laws and nature of that great Being in Whom we live
and move and have our being will be studied.[22]

The Theosophist's perennial philosophy is first and foremost a
spiritual anthropogeny and cosmogony. As we are just beginning to
explore material space, so what Bailey is looking forward to is a time
when we will start to explore esoteric space (the staring-us-in-the-face
reality seen when the veil is lifted). Then we will 'in deed and in truth'
be cosmologists. The entirety of this universe might be pictured as a
circle with a central dot, that dot itself being a circle with another
central dot, and so on ad infinitum. Each circle is the range of a consciousness, with the greater consciousness including the lesser but,
says Theosophy, evolutions on different logoic-system levels are
somehow related. The liberation of each individual man from the
limitations of its form does its small part to release our Solar Man
from the limitations of Its form, taught Bailey.

'I see the universe as a hierarchy of levels descending from the
formless spiritual level down to the most dense material form', wrote
Philip Sherrard.[23] Blavatsky wrote: 'Spirit is Matter *on the seventh
plane*; Matter is Spirit – on the lowest point of its cyclic activity; and

both – are Maya.'[24] As evolution proceeds, man 'leaves behind' identifications with his only-apparently-real physical existence, then his only-apparently-real emotional existence, and so on, and these bodies – in some static picture at least – partake of the substance (looking upwards) of progressively less 'material' levels. But all is Maya, as the body of our God is only relatively real (as we consider the higher system He is in), and there is *a simultaneity of activity of logoic-systems* (circle with a dot, that dot a circle with a dot ...). Three-dimensionalizing this picture, we have here the meaning to Blavatsky's words: 'It is on the doctrine of the illusive nature of Matter, and the infinite divisibility of the *Atom,* that the whole Science of Occultism is built.'[25] Also: 'Every atom in the Universe has the potentiality of self-consciousness in it, and is ... a Universe in itself, and *for* itself.'[26]

THE SEVEN SPIRITS

Looking at things from where we 'ordinarily are', in terms of consciousness, at the end of evolution our consciousness develops into one 'off our scale'. The journey, says Theosophy, sees us dis-identify with all our bodies – the sheaths or 'principles' of man. Seven of these are normally listed, and there is a connection between these and the initiations, which is explored in Part Two. Another septenary in Theosophical writings is the 'Sacred Planets' (the same Saturn, Jupiter, Mars, the Sun, Venus, Mercury, and the Moon, that were related in some way to the Gnostic Archons). Is there a connection? According to Hall, the planetary names just listed are the *symbolic* names for the principles in the archaic (Gnostic-Hermetic) Mysteries. 'Uninitiated mortals exist in physical natures limited to the concerns of the earth', he wrote, and 'the corporeal body [which is not a principle] was transmuted by the Mysteries into a celestial body.'[27] Above *this* earth are *these* planets and above these the stars. (Above the stars is the *Empyrean* of the ancients – the highest cosmic heaven. One of the Hermetic texts is called *The Discourse on the Eighth and the Ninth,* and the 'Eighth' refers to the level of the stars above the 'mesocosm' or Hebdomad of the planetary range, whilst the 'Ninth' refers to the Empyrean.[28])

In his book *The Doctrine of the Spheres*, Purucker says that as we 'wing our way sunwards', we shall leave what we took from each of the seven Sacred Planets.[29] What we 'took' would then be our existence *as* the bodies/sheaths/principles – seven in all. Another term we find in Theosophical writings is 'Planetary Spirits' (of which there are seven), and also – particularly in the writings of Bailey – 'Rays' (seven again). Bailey says that the Rays are the centres in the body of our God: they are *body-consciousness centres* then. Jacob Boehme wrote of 'Seven Spirits' which he likened to wheels ceaselessly turning. If the body-consciousness of a higher being is the Aevertinal reality, then these Rays/Spirits would be always there too. Here are the Archons 'in themselves', correlating to the Gods, just beneath God, in an our-cosmos-system-only Great Chain of Being.

Quantitatively or empirically of course, we see today our solar system made up of a physical sun and nine (or ten) planets; also their sixty-one moons (including the Earth's), asteroids, comets, and inter-stellar dust. There would appear to be a numerical and taxonomical 'gap' here then. Not so, says Theosophy. The confusion is understand-able, but as the centres are body-consciousness centres, and each cosmos-system (on whatever logoic-system level) is a body-con-sciousness of some being, so every being finds itself in a manifestation as the realm of *some* seven 'Archons'. There are thus solar Rays (including *our* solar Rays), and cosmic Rays (including *our* cosmic Rays). It is possible that these 'Seven' also relate to the *chakras* in Eastern psyche-ology (crown, forehead, heart, throat, solar plexus, sacrum, and base of spine). Bailey certainly invites us to consider the following correspondences or relationships:

FIGURE 4: OUR COSMOS-SYSTEM GREAT CHAIN OF BEING

Name of Solar Plane	Principle/ Chakra	Great Chain of Being	'Type' of Consciousness
Divine	None	God	Solar
Monadic	The Monad/ Crown (synthesis of others)	Gods	Planetary
Atmic or Nirvanic	Atma/ Forehead	Angels	Spiritual 2
Buddhic	Buddhi/ Heart	Sages	Spiritual 1
(Higher) Mental or Manasic (Lower)	Manas/ Throat Kama Manas/ Solar Plexus	(On the Path) Human Beings (Ordinary)	Human
Emotional	Astral/ Sacral	Animals	Animal
(Etheric) Physical (Dense)	Etheric/ Base of Spine	Plants Rocks	Vegetable Mineral

Atma-Buddhi-Manas = The 'Ternary'
Kama Manas-Astral-Etheric-Dense = The 'Quaternary'

4 Some Other Esoteric Schools

CHRISTIAN THEOSOPHY

> The Work is not the Atonement of Reconciliation, but it is
> the Building which the true Spirit buildeth in his
> Substance; it is his Habitation.
>
> Jacob Boehme[1]

Christian Theosophy is the name given to the train of theosophical thought that passes through Jacob Boehme (1575-1624), and his successors such as John Pordage (1608-1681) and Jane Leade (1624-1704) – co-founders of the Philadelphian Society, Johann Georg Gichtel (1638-1710), Friedrich Christoph Oetinger (1702-1782) and Franz von Baader (1765-1841). The stream did not originate with Boehme: its source can be traced back through Christian mystics such as Meister Eckhart (c1260-c1327), John Scotus Erigena (c810-c877), and Pseudo-Dionysius the Areopagite (c 6th century), to the Christian Gnostics of the first few centuries. We also note the 'Christian Alchemist', Valentin Weigel (1533-1588) and the 'Christian Hermeticists', Lodovico Lazzarelli (1447-1500) and Francesco Patrizi (1529-1597). If Sufism represents Islamic esotericism, and Kabbalism represents Jewish esotericism, then Christian

Theosophy – including Christian Gnosticism – represents the tradition of Christian esotericism.

There is certainly a Christic element in the Theosophy of Blavatsky, Bailey, etc., but aside from the difference of the Eastern terminological imports, there is also the distinction in the 'non-aligned' Theosophy of the person of Christ being, well, more of a person. A high initiate to be sure (seventh or eighth is maintained), but still essentially 'one of us'. In Christian Theosophy, the person of Christ tends to remain supremely venerable, whereas in Modern Theosophy, Christ is brought back down to Earth somewhat (which is to say to our cosmos-system only), as merely a senior figure in the Lodge. We find something approximating the Lodge in Christian Theosophy: Leade wrote of a 'Coelestial University' populated by teachers who possessed 'clarified bodies' and who taught the 'new Science' of the 'Angelical Philosophy'.[2]

We have already made mention of Boehme's Seven Spirits, which we have identified with Bailey's Rays and the Gnostic Archons. The Seven Spirits are the 'generated images of the Trinity', that are 'reflected in the seven planetary qualities', says Arthur Versluis.[3] Boehme's Trinity and ultimate God, as we read in the following quote from him, appear identical to the Gnostic Logos coupled with the Traditionalist's Absolute: 'God is the eternal One, or the greatest stillness, so far as he exists to himself independently of his motion and manifestation. But in his motion he is called a God in Trinity.'[4] The 'stillness' here is the Absolute – what Boehme calls the Abyss or *Ungrund*. It is the *supra*ontological, hence 'un, ground. 'Motion' here reminds us of our earlier definition of a Logos as an engine of imagination.

Christian Theosophy affirms the Great Work in its own language: as spiritual regeneration. There is a building work to do – of the individual's own 'Temple of Christ'. There is a seven-stage 'dark valley' of creation, as the levels are put in place one by one along the Hermetic line; we are born, and then we need to be reborn into the 'life of Christ'. There are actually *three* births. The first is the natural or 'outward' birth, the second is the birth of the soul in the human consciousness, and the third is the birth of the spirit or the highest divinity

33

in the soul. In Christian Theosophy man – every man – is body, soul, and spirit, and the three births relate to each of these. At the end of the road, man sees through his highest spiritual eye. This 'eye in the heart' (a phrase also popular with Frithjof Schuon) was/is the eye 'with which God sees himself through us', says Versluis.[5] The Fall of Man (or Adam) is a moving away from this higher (Aevertinal) consciousness to a lower (Character or earthly man) consciousness, so that instead of seeing transcendent reality, we see only the temporophysical world. However, we cannot think of it as a *personal* fall – how could it be, when it is creation which brings the very person(al) into being?

Magia and the Supersensual Way

Boehme wrote: 'Magic is the greatest secrecy, for it is above Nature [manifestation], and makes Nature after the form of its will. It is the mystery of the Ternary, viz. it is in desire the will striving towards the heart of God.'[6] God's Will in Christian Theosophy is *magia* (magic), which *post*-creation is to ascend/evolve, and *pre*-creation is to descend/involve. God wishes to know himself (speaking here of the 'Unknown God' – the Absolute), and he does this through means of the Trinity, producing the logoic system. Boehme's treatise *The Supersensual Life* (1622), is in the form of a dialogue between a spiritual disciple and his master. The disciple asks his master how he may come to know God. His master replies: 'When thou standest still from the thinking of self, and the willing of self [the personal self] ... then the Eternal Hearing, Seeing, and Speaking will be revealed in thee.'[7] He goes on to say how 'it is nought indeed but thine own Hearing and Willing that do hinder thee [keeping the veil in place], so that thou dost not see and hear God.'[8] There must be an unmaking of our ordinary consciousness, and an 'entire Surrender and yielding up of thy Will', so that 'the Love of God in thee becometh the Life of thy Nature.'[9]

Such a life is one of a true vision-of-things, a responsibility to do the Right Thing which is born out of this, and a felicity in doing so, for we are finally 'living up to ourselves' (as Christ did). Along the Supersensual Way, there is the transformation from an 'unconscious life pulled and pushed by emotional tides' (what Blavatsky and Bailey would have called 'astralism') to 'a conscious life lived in the light of the Divine', says Versluis.[10] 'All Christian Religion', wrote Boehme, in *Of Regeneration, or the New Birth* (1622), 'wholly consisteth in this, to learn *to know ourselves*; whence we are come and what we are.'[11] The difference between the understanding of the theologian and the theosopher (reminding us of Schuon's words), is the recognition by the latter that understanding of God must come from the 'Interior Fountain' and enter the mind from the Christ nature *within the Soul*. Unless this takes place, all teaching about divine things is useless and worthless. Along the Supersensual Way there is a stage called the 'Wedding of the Lamb', which, as we shall see, corresponds to the marriage of the man and his silver nature in Alchemy. 'We heartily wish', wrote Boehme, 'that the titular and Lip-Christians might once find by Experience in themselves [this Wedding], and so pass from the History into the Substance'.[12]

KABBALISM

'With specific regard to spiritual evolution, there is an apparent parallel between Blavatskyan Theosophy, the Kabbalah, and ... Christian Theosophy', writes Nicholas Goodrick-Clarke[13]. The word 'Kabbalah' comes from *Kabal* meaning 'to receive', and as the Neoplatonists recognized a line of Wisdom-teachers, so too did the Kabbalists – the latter's line passing through Abraham, Moses, and Jesus. The *Shalshelet ha-Kabbalah* ('Chain of Esoteric Tradition') is grounded in the Aevertinal, and the 'Way of the Kabbalah' – also the 'Work of the Chariot' and the Redemption (*Tiqqun*) is the spiritual path. The three main Kabbalistic texts are the *Sepher Zohar* ('Book of Splendour'), written – or at least written *down* – by Moses de Leon (1240-1305), although the 2nd century Simeon bar Yohai is also credited with its authorship; the *Sepher Bahir* ('Book of Illumination'), which appeared in France in the 12th century, but is attributed to the 1st century Rabbi Nehunia ben HaKanah; and the *Sepher Yetzirah* ('Book of Formation'), whose legendary author was Abraham, but which may

35

have been written around the same time as the *Bahir* (perhaps by Akiba ben Joseph, who wrote of his journey through the 'Seven Heavenly Halls'). The main metaphysical characters in Kabbalism are the Infinite *Ain Soph* and the ten (or occasionally eleven) *Sephiroth*.

Kabbalism passed into Europe through, amongst others, Aaron ben Samuel (9th century), Solomon ibn Gabirol (c1021-c1088) – whose work fused the teachings of Kabbalism, Sufism, and Neoplatonism, Abraham Abulafia (1240-1291), and Joseph ben Abraham Gikatilla (1248-c1325). Particularly after the expulsion of the Jews from Spain in 1492, Kabbalism was a major thought-player in Europe in the 15th to 18th centuries, co-mingling with the 're-discovered' Hermeticism and Neoplatonism, together with Alchemy and the Christian theo-sophical stream. One product of this was a *Christian* Kabbalism associated with such names as Giovanni Pico della Mirandola (1463-1494), Johannes Trithemius (1462-1516), Johann Reuchlin (1455-1522), Guillaume Postel (1510-1581), Robert Fludd (1574-1637), and Christian Knorr von Rosenroth (1636-1689). Two major *maggids* (teachers) of Jewish Kabbalism in the 16th century were Moses ben Jacob Cordovero (1522-1570), and Isaac Luria (1534-1572). Later teachers of Jewish Kabbalism included Israel ben Eleazer (1698-1760) – founder of the Hasidic movement, Moses Hayyim Luzzatto (1707-1747), and, in the last century, Yehuda Ashlag (1885-1955). Kabbalism was one of the three main sources (the other two being Alchemy and Hermeticism) of the teachings of Eliphas Levi (1810-1875) and Aleister Crowley (1875-1947), and the latter specifically linked the grades of occult initiation to the Sephiroth. For Gershom Scholem, there may have been a Zoharic source behind Blavatsky's *The Secret Doctrine*.[14]

> *Three Supreme Sephiroth:*
> *Kether* ('Crown')
> *Chokmah* ('Wisdom')
> *Binah* ('Understanding')

Seven Lower Sephiroth:
> *Chesed* ('Compassion')
> *Geburah* ('Strength')
> *Tiphereth* ('Beauty')
> *Netsah* ('Triumph')
> *Hod* ('Majesty')
> *Jesod* ('Foundation')
> *Malkuth* ('Kingdom')

Concerning the Sephiroth, writes Leo Schaya, 'a prefiguration of the Christian Trinity may be found in the three supreme Sephiroth … whereas in the other seven Sephiroth, which are of an onto-cosmological nature, we discover the Trinity in that it descends towards the cosmos.'[15] Ain Soph – the 'Lord Superlatively One' – has a supraontological unity, as does Boehme's Hidden God, and this Absolute can be symbolized as a circle *before* the Hermeticist's spirit-dot. What would constitute the 'dot' in Kabbalism would then be the first Sephirah, Kether, or the 'Kabbalistic Trinity' of Kether, Chokmah, and Binah. Sephiroth can be defined as 'vessels', and more than one author has identified the lower seven Sephiroth with the Eastern chakras. Kabbalism, like Christian Theosophy, also strongly attests that man is body, soul, and spirit (*nefesh*, *ruach*, and *neshamah* respectively), and commonly speaks of four worlds (from bottom to top: *Assiah*, *Yetzirah*, *Briah* and *Atziluth*). Sometimes a fifth, the world of *Adam Kadmon*, is added above the world of Atziluth.

> *In Kabbalism:*
> Atziluth ('World of Emanation')
> Briah ('World of Creation')
> Yetzirah ('World of Formation')
> Assiah ('World of Manifestation')

> *In Sufism:*
> *Alam al-Izzah* ('World of Glory')
> *Alam al-Jabarut* ('World of Power')

Alam al-Malakut ('World of Royalty')
Alam al-Mulk ('World of Possession')

These worlds are worlds of *experience*. Assiah is the world of ordinary experience. It is 'this world of man and matter' – the Traditionalists' quantitative dimension. It is more than just the *material* universe, for it would also include the Theosophists' emotional and lower mental levels too. There is a 'Gestation' period along the Way of the Kabbalah, writes Z'ev ben Shimon Halevi.[16] Before the time of 'Awakening Consciousness', when the student *now* has a *mystical* interpretation of the Kabbalah, he is limited to a literal, allegorical, or metaphysical inter-pretation of it – as he is limited to the Assiah world of experience. Theosophists read into the Sephiroth foursome Malkuth, Jesod, Hod, and Netsah, the Quaternary of physical, etheric, emotional, and lower mental centres. What the student awakens to after this 'Gestation' *is* experience of the world of Yetzirah, says Halevi, and this relates to the 'soul triad' of Tiphereth, Geburah, and Chesed (which the Theosophists link with the Ternary of higher mental, buddhic, and atmic centres). Following 'Awakening', there is the period of 'Nourishment', and following this there is the period of 'Maturity', which leads into experience of the world of Briah. On paper, Yetzirah is the abode of men's souls, and Briah is the abode of Heaven. In Heaven are the 'Elders of the House of Israel' instructed by one 'fully developed Man'. Of the latter, Halevi writes: 'To some he is known as the Messiah and to others the Axis of an Age. He has a place and name in every living Tradition.'[17] Atziluth is the 'unchanging divine world', and might therefore relate to the Theosophists' Pure Consciousness (and the sharing in the body-consciousness of our Solar Man). If so, then the world of Adam Kadmon might relate to our Solar Man on cosmic levels.

The lower seven Sephiroth have been linked with the biblical figures of (reading upwards) David, Joseph, Aaron, Moses, Jacob, Isaac, and Abraham; and Franz Bardon linked these – together with Binah – to the unprincipled Earth (0), the Moon (1), Mercury (2), Venus (3), the Sun (4), Mars (5), Jupiter (6), and Saturn (7) in the archaic Mysteries. Chokmah and Kether would then relate to the

Ogdoad (8) and Ennead (9) respectively, leaving Ain Soph to claim the 'Tenth'. We note that the Sun here links to Tiphereth, which in virtually all interpretations of the Kabbalah has a central role as the soul, or more specifically, as the soul *body* (the 'Seat of Solomon'). This is homologous to the *Temple* of Solomon in esoteric Free-masonry, and the Causal Body in Theosophy (see next Part). Two other terms we find in Kabbalism are *Macroprosophus* (the 'Great Face'), which relates to the Kabbalists' spirit-dot; and *Microprosophus* (the 'Lesser Face'), which relates to the lower Sephiroth, minus the 'unprincipled' Malkuth. The Lesser Face is symbolized by the six-pointed star: here is the marriage of the threefold lower man (Jesod, Hod, and Netsah), with the threefold higher man (Tiphereth, Geburah, and Chesed). Kabbalism, like Christian Theosophy, also emphasizes the *Will*. Says Yehuda Ashlag on this:

> By creation of the worlds, with their involutions down to this mundane world, a proper place is prepared for divine service … (not for the purpose of meriting a reward, but for the sole purpose of imparting delight to the Creator). Souls then become fit to invert their will to receive (which severs and separates them from the Creator) into a will to impart (which resembles the will of the Creator) and by this means to attain the highest degree of devotion and unity. As that stage of unity is reached by souls, their will to receive has already been stripped from them, for they have acquired instead a will to impart. They become altruists instead of egotists. The will to bestow is like the will of the Creator, Himself.[18]

ALCHEMY

All Hermetic Philosophers say that, although the Ars Magna is a natural thing, both in its essence and in its operations, yet things so surprising take place in it, that they elevate the spirit of man toward the Author of his being, that they might manifest His wisdom and glory.

Antoine-Joseph Pernety[19]

Alchemy is a practice, not a school, but we can speak of a tradition of alchemical thought. To say 'in Alchemy' we therefore mean in alchemical thought, and here we are considering that thought: a) in the West (chiefly from the 13th to 17th centuries); and b) on 'inner' or spiritual alchemy (*Neidan* in the Chinese tradition), as opposed to 'outer' or material alchemy. The material and spiritual alchemist alike seek to transmute lead (or base metals generally) into silver and gold, but for the latter, the 'lead' is himself and 'silver' and 'gold' relate to 'his' soul and spirit natures respectively. Names associated with Western Alchemy – Alchemy in Europe – include Raymond Lull (1235-1310), Nicholas Flamel (1330-1417), Bernard of Treves (1406-1490), Marsilio Ficino (1433-1499) and Heinrich Khunrath (1560-1605). We can also add to this list Paracelsus (and his legendary teacher Salomen Trismosin), Agrippa, Fludd, Gichtel, and Weigel.[20]

The spiritual-alchemical work is the Ars Magna, the Great Work, the Royal Road, and the Hermetic Art. As the Royal Road, it is also the knightly quest and the work of kings. This work, says Titus Burckhardt, is to 'regain the original nobility of human nature'.[21] 'Original' here refers to the Traditionalists' Aevertinal, and the work is therefore one that leads upwards to Pure Consciousness and the individual status of *Zhenren* ('Authentic Man') in Chinese Alchemy. The Hermetic Art is the art of negotiating the ascent through the planetary spheres (the Great Work is also the *Solar Work*) and, at the same time as being an art, it is a 'natural science'. It can be such when the Way is both *natural* (the Neoplatonists' entelechy), and the procedure is not vague and haphazard but *systematic*. In Western Alchemy, we see the body, soul, and spirit represented by salt, mercury, and sulphur. We also see the soul symbolized by the Queen, and the spirit by the King. If we can speak of a world-picture of Alchemy, it would be the Ptolemaic, with the earth at the centre (or the bottom), then around this (or next up) are the planets, then around these (or next up again) are the stars, and then the Empyrean. 'The alchemist [in his ascent] *reverses cosmogony*' offers Maurice Aniane,[22] and Julius Evola asserts that the alchemical initiation experience 'furnishes the key to cosmogony'.[23]

Read Downwards = Cosmogony
Read Upwards = Ars Magna:
Cosmic
Solar
Planetary
Earthly

Alchemists speak of a *Philosopher's Stone*. This usually has the same meaning as the Temple of Christ in Christian Theosophy. The King is also the Red Lion and the Queen the White Eagle, where the body (the personal self) is the Black Crow. (There is an abundance of images and symbols in Alchemy – these are just some of the more common.) The three generally recognized stages of the Work are 'the Black' (*Nigredo*), 'the White' (*Albedo*), and 'the Red' (*Rubedo*). There is also reference to the 'Work of the Night', the 'Work of the Dawn', and the 'Work of the Day'. It is clear that the Black stage (which involves a 'Putrefaction'), refers to the death of the personal ego – or more specifically, the death of the *identification with* the personal ego. Putrefaction is the 'existential death, the loss of personal identity', says Antoine Faivre.[24] Titus Burckhardt prefers to speak only of *two* stages: 1) from Black to White; and 2) from White to Red. The first of these (which is also the 'Lesser Work'), has to do with the 'spiritualization of the body'; and the second (the 'Greater Work'), has to do with the 'embodying of the spirit'.[25] He writes: 'Whereas the "lesser work" has as its goal the regaining of the original purity and receptivity of the *soul*, the goal of the "greater work" is the illumination of the soul by the revelation of the *Spirit* within it.'[26]

In the next part we will consider the two broad stages of the spiritual path in esotericism, which are 'from personality to soul' and 'from soul to spirit'. The first of these covers the period up to the third occult initiation, and the second covers the period from there up to the fifth initiation at least. Alchemists speak of a Divine Marriage of the opposites; also of a 'Chymical Wedding'. There are actually *two* 'marriages' along the Way. The first is between the alchemist and his silver (soul) nature, and the second is between the silvered alchemist and his gold (spirit) nature. We see that the soul (the Queen) can be thought of as 'female', and if there *was* just the Lesser Work, then there would be just the one marriage – between the 'male' personal ego and the Queen (also Luna). Aniane speaks of this first marriage as that in which 'cosmic femininity prevails over masculine objectivity'.[27]

But there is also a Greater Work, and therefore a higher marriage – between the Queen and a King (who is also Sol). The Queen is in addition represented by Aurora, the Roman goddess of the dawn, whose brother is Helios the Sun. (This marriage is also the 'Hierosgamos of the Sun and the Moon', and the 'Conjunctio of Fire and Water'.) *And yet further*, there is a death and resurrection of this 'Hermetic Androgyne'. The first marriage, the second marriage, and the final resurrection, relate to the Theosophists' third, fifth, and seventh initiations, as we shall see in the next part. Seven grades of initiation are, indeed, often mentioned in Alchemy. Recalling our division of earthly, planetary, solar, and cosmic, at the first initiation the alchemist may be said to leave the earthly realm and begin his journey through the planetary realm. At the seventh initiation, he leaves the planetary realm and enters the solar realm – hence the reversal of cosmogony.

In *The Six Keys of Eudoxus*, an anonymous 17th century text, there is a First Work, a Second Work, *and* a Third Work. The First Work (which the author of this text breaks down into three stages or 'Keys') is to 'whiten the Black, and vivify the White', and during this the 'Wise Artist cuts off the head of the Black Dragon'.[28] The Black Dragon represents the ordinary analytical mind that, by itself, cannot escape its own gravity. The First Work ends with the marriage of the man and the Queen. We now have our Philosopher's Stone, and following this the Philosophers 'rubefied the white stone with the solar sperm', wrote Marsilio Ficino.[29] The Second Work (after two more Keys) ends with the marriage of the Queen/silvered man and the King. The Third Work relates to the period after the fifth initiation, which, as this is the period after relative enlightenment (again, dealt with in the next part), is the Work of the Day.

FIGURE 5: THE ALCHEMICAL WORK

Work:	Leading to:
First or Night Work	Marriage of the man (the personality) and the Queen (the soul)
Keys 1-3	Also the making of the Philosopher's Stone
From Black to White	This period involves a Putrefaction and a Whitening work

Painfully, quietly, he [the Alchemist] re-collects it [his soul nature] in himself as still water. He brings Mercury back to its indeterminate possibility: this is the 'return to materia prima'.

Maurice Aniane[30]

Second or Dawn Work	Marriage of the silvered alchemist and the King (the spirit)
Keys 4-5	Also the production of the Golden Elixir (*Jindan* in
From White to Red	Chinese Alchemy)

The Fourth Key of the Art is the entrance to the Second Work ... The terrification of the Spirit is the only operation of this work ... To corporify the Spirit ... you must have well dissolved the body [the Stone] in which the sulphur is enclosed.

Eudoxus[31]

Third or Day Work	The Final Resurrection
Keys 6+	Some Alchemists speak of 'the Purple' stage – the royal
Post-Red	colour at the end of the Royal Road or Solar Work. Here we have a 'Vivification' and a 'Multiplication' of the spiritual light; also a 'Projection of the Medicine' into the world.[32]

The whole Progress of the Philosopher's work is nothing but Solution [dissolving] of the body [the personal ego], and Congelation [establishing, reifying] of the Spirit [for the good of all].

Jean d'Espagnet[33]

PART TWO

THE SPIRITUAL PATH

5 Spirituality and Cosmology

SPIRITUALITY AND INITIATION

> The first necessity for obtaining self-knowledge is to become profoundly conscious of ignorance; to feel with every fibre of the heart that one is ceaselessly self-deceived. The second requisite is the still deeper conviction that such knowledge … can be obtained by effort. The third and most important is an indomitable determination to obtain and face that.
>
> Helena Blavatsky[1]

In this part we will consider the spiritual or initiatory path as expressed chiefly in the modern theosophical language (that is, in the language of Blavatsky, Purucker, Bailey, etc. – and we will welcome Rudolf Steiner in this part too). The reader might therefore wish to re-read Chapter 3 at this point. Modern Theosophy is the most recent and comparativistic esoteric school, and its language is arguably at once more accessible and technically complete. In any event, there is a dearth of material on the specifics of the Path in many other esoteric schools (the exception perhaps being Kabbalism). We will consider ideas on what the path is, the stages of it, its relation to the planes, the Rays/Spirits and the principles, and the work that the individual has to do – and why. We might begin by noting that the phrase 'path of initiation' is often used and that this path is, in the words of Bailey, a 'self-chosen forcing process'.[2] Max Heindel writes that the path is an opportunity to develop the higher faculties in a short time and by severe training, 'thereby gaining the expansion of consciousness that all mankind will surely possess eventually, but which the vast majority choose to acquire through the slow process of ordinary evolution'.[3] The spiritual path as the path of initiation, is the 'short-cut' route of the spiritually aspiring. *To* initiate is to cause a process or action to begin. *The* initiate, says Bailey, is not the *result* of the evolutionary process, but is the *cause* of it, and by means of it he perfects his vehicles of spiritual expression.

We commonly speak of being initiated into a group (which may involve the taking of an oath, or the performing of a ritual), or of being initiated into an experience. It is in the latter sense that we re-cognize the 'natural' initiations such as the transition from childhood to adulthood, and the social or cultural initiations that may accom-pany these. But as Robert Ellwood says, there is also a third type of initiation – the spiritual – recognized by most religious traditions.[4] (As we have used the fictional world of Middle Earth as an analogy for our ontological-existential situation, it should be noted here that Ellwood has used *The Lord of the Rings* story as a spiritual path alle-gory.[5]) A spiritual initiation is a *breakthrough into a new awareness*, with the spiritual path being divided into stages, each of which follows one breakthrough in awareness, and leads up to another. This point is to be emphasized: 'No initiation can be conferred upon another', says Purucker. 'All growth, all spiritual illumination, takes place *within oneself*.'[6] And the Rosicrucianist R Swinburne Clymer stresses:

> Occult Initiation is not to be confused with ordinary ceremonial initiation, however beautifully illustrative it may be. Occult Initiation is the gradual revelation of the Mysteries to the Soul as it gains interior *Consciousness* of its Divinity or Immortality.[7]

Why would a person choose to undergo this 'severe training'? Ultimately, perhaps, because he *must* – referring to a soteriologicalexistential need. Ellwood says that the turning point in an individual's life where he decides to undergo this training normally follows a period of deep despair at the meaninglessness or emptiness of ordinary life.[8] Alternatively, it may be after a steadily deepening intellectual interest with years of study and reflection, culminating in a 'philosophically necessary' decision to cease mere intellectualizing. Annie Besant says that repeated longings for earthly pleasures and intellectual gratifications, followed by full possession and subsequent weariness, gradually teach the individual the transient and unsatisfactory nature of ordinary life's gifts. He now says to himself:

> All is vanity and vexation. Hundreds, yea, thousands of times have I possessed, and finally have found disappointment even in possession. These joys are illusions, as bubbles on the stream, airy-coloured, rainbow-hued, but bursting at a touch. I am athirst for realities; I have had enough of shadows; I pant for the eternal and the true, for freedom from the limitations that hem me in, that keep me a prisoner amid these changing shows.[9]

Theosophy teaches that the journey sees us dis-identify with all our bodies. The Monad is the seventh (counting upwards), and Monadic consciousness refers to the sharing in the body-consciousness of our Planetary Man. This is the 'first' God we meet and therefore, to some degree or up to a point, the only one that we need concern ourselves with. Indeed, says Theosophy, when God is spoken of in mystical traditions, it is *this* God that is commonly being referred to. *Enlightenment*, therefore, generally refers to a sharing in a planetary consciousness – *not* a whole-universe consciousness, although it is not 'incorrect' to speak of this God as *the* God, *the* Whole, because it is our *initial* ontological-cosmogenetic 'context'. In Theosophy, there are five initiations sometimes called (with a nod to Christian mysticism) the Birth, the Baptism, the Transfiguration, the Crucifixion, and the Resurrection. (The last of these is alternatively called the Revelation, with the *seventh* initiation being the true Resurrection.) These five initiations stand between ordinary human consciousness and the sharing in the body-consciousness of our Planetary Man as God. *This* enlightenment not being the end of things though, there are yet two higher initiations that may be taken in or in relation to our cosmos-system. 'There are actually ten degrees', says Purucker, 'but only the seven that pertain to the seven manifested planes of the solar system need concern us.'[10]

Five, seven, ten initiations … the author has followed the common Theosophical division of the path in this part – a division based on the ubiquitous 'lower seven' and the 'higher three'. Different numerical divisions are possible and proffered though – Bailey, for instance, sometimes refers to the Transfiguration as the *first* major initiation, on account of gnosis now taking on a *cosmological* character (it always had a cosmological *context*). The second major initiation is then the fifth in the common division – a wider cosmological dimension begins to open up here (solar and not merely planetary). The first of these major initiations corresponds with the 'appearance of the gold' at the end of the alchemical Work of the Night, and the second corresponds with the Hierosgamos of the Sun and the Moon at the end of the Work of the Dawn. Then again, the 'Threshold' in esoteric Freemasonry is not crossed until the arrival of 'the Day': the first instalment of a genuinely new life awaits this. We mustn't get too hung up on the numerical division then, although there is no relativity when it comes to the *direction* of the path. As Steiner once said, ultimately the path is the path from the spiritual in us to the spiritual *in the universe*.

The next chapter of this part will consider the first initiation, which Theosophists believe humanity in general (or a significant proportion of it) is approaching. This collective breakthrough will 'influence the development of world society in a significant way', says Niels Bronsted,[11] an understatement if it is true. Chapter 7 will consider the second and third initiations, Chapter 8 the fourth and fifth initiations, and Chapter 9 the higher initiations (sixth, seventh, and beyond). As we consider all of these, we will have the opportunity to relate them to the stages of meditation in Raja Yoga, and also to the three common mystical experiences identified by Robert K C Forman (the Pure Consciousness Event, the Dualistic Mystical State, and the Unitive Mystical State), and the Dark Night of the Soul, and the Unitive Life according to Evelyn Underhill. In Part Three, which also deals with 'regular' spiritual psychology, we will have the opportunity to relate the initiations to the higher (transpersonal) stages of consciousness evolution as posited by Ken Wilber. To conclude this chapter, we will continue with some more general thoughts on the spiritual or initiatory path.

INITIATOLOGY AND COSMOLOGY

The path, writes J S Bakula, 'initiates an individual into the higher and expanded states of consciousness associated with the planes of the top half'.[12] These would be the planes above the physical, emotional, and lower mental. If we could somehow make a robot like us, in terms of our 'consciousness predicament', then the robot would be in a position to know/be himself as a thinker, feeler, and actor – as we are. In Theosophy, we are in a position to know/be ourselves as thinkers, feelers, and actors because – as it is normally expressed – our lowest principles or chakra centres are *open*. But the Adept (the fifth initiate) has all seven centres open, which means he is in a position to know/be himself as more than just a thinker, feeler, and actor. *Normally*, says Niels Bronsted (with the understanding that things do not always go like this – Steiner also speaks of this[13]), at the first initiation the throat (manas) centre is opened; at the second initiation the heart (buddhi) centre is opened; and at the third initiation the two head centres (atma and the Monad) are opened.

At the third initiation, says Bronsted, 'the disciple has his first direct contact with the Monad … the planetary Logos himself functioning through his vehicle of expression.'[14] The word 'first' is important here. Swami Rajarshi Muni, writing on the stages in the life of the yogi, speaks of a time in which the individual experiences the 'distant and serenely blissful reflection of his or her atman [Monad], which gradually becomes clearer and clearer'.[15] 'Clearer and clearer' would refer to the fourth and fifth initiations, when Monadic consciousness becomes more fully the possession of the individual. In relation to the third initiation, perhaps, Jiddu Krishnamurti described the following numinous experience:

> On the first day while I was in that state and more conscious of things around me, I had the most extraordinary experience. There was a man mending the road; that man was myself; the pickaxe he held was myself; the very stone which he was breaking up was a part of me; the tender blade of grass was my very being, and the tree beside the man was myself. I also could feel and think like the road mender and I could feel the wind passing through the trees, and the little ant on the blade of grass I could feel. The birds, the dust and the very noise were a part of me. Just then there was a car passing by at some distance; I was the driver, the engine, and the tires; as the car went further away from me, I was going away from myself. I was in everything, or rather everything was in me, inanimate and animate, the mountain, the worm and all breathing things.[16]

Esotericists teach that man is a threefold being – body, soul, and spirit. In Gnostic terms, hyle, psyche, and pneuma, and in Kabbalistic terms, nefesh, ruach, and neshamah. Spirit here *can* refer to the Monad, and body to the corporate personal ego (the personality – the thinker, feeler, and actor). Man identifies first with the circle, then with the line, then with the dot, say the Hermeticists, so the sequence is: identification with the body (the personal ego/personality), identification with the soul (consciousness), identification with the spirit (Monad). The spiritual path may be divided into two halves. The first half (up to the third initiation) is about going from the first to the second of these – from personality to soul. The second half (from the third initiation up to the fifth initiation at least) is about going from soul to spirit.

> For all there are two stages of the path … The first degree is the conversion from the lower life; the second – held by

those that have already made their way to the sphere of the
Intelligibles, have set as it were a footprint there but must
still advance within the realm – lasts until they reach the
extreme hold of the place, the Term attained when the
topmost peak of the Intellectual realm is won.

Plotinus[17]

The personal ego/personality does not 'evaporate' as such. It is about
becoming a new *one*self, as opposed to a new *other* self. 'Men fear such
a path because they fear the loss of personality, which is to them life
itself', says Paul Brunton. 'But the exact truth is that the personal ego
is [simply] subordinated, turned into an agent for a higher power.'[18]
The man becomes an agent of the Divine – in another language, the
'Son of the Father' – and his spiritual service has to do with the heavenization of the world. In performing this he has what we might call
'spiritual job satisfaction', and is what G I Gurdjieff (like the Chinese
Alchemists) would call an authentic man or woman. In Boehme's
The Supersensual Life, the Disciple asks: 'Will not the Light of Nature
in me be extinguished by this greater Light [of God]?' The Master
replies:

By no Means at all. It is true, the evil Nature will be
destroyed by It; but by the Destruction thereof you can be
no Loser, but very much a Gainer. The Eternal Band of
Nature is the same afterward as before; and the Properties
are the same. So that Nature hereby is only advanced and
meliorated; and the Light thereof, or human Reason, by
being kept within its due Bounds, and regulated by a
superior Light is only made useful.[19]

We might return to the Middle Earth analogy in an attempt to aid our
'technical' understanding of the spiritual path – and indeed the whole
cosmos-system we find ourselves in. The physical plane of this world
would be made up of all the physical bodies of the rocks, plants, animals, and human(oid) characters such as Mr Baggins that populate it.

The emotional plane would be made up of all the emotional bodies – the feeling natures – of the characters and animals. When Mr Baggins looks at his friends, he doesn't just see physical beings before him, even if this is what his scientific instruments, or his culture's materialist philosophy (if such it had), tell him alone exists. He would see people who feel, like him, and if he could bag these feeling natures, he would have in his bag his friends' emotional bodies. His mount also feels, and therefore has an emotional body too. His friends (but not his mount) also think, like him, and the mental plane would be made up of all the mental bodies (the intellects) of himself, his friends, and all the other characters.

But Middle Earth only exists in an author's imagination. So, if we were entering Middle Earth (with our knowledge of this), and meeting Mr Baggins (who, as far is he is concerned, is real and so is his world), we might say to him that the reality he sees is relatively real, but behind it is a 'spiritual creative energy'. Esotericism teaches that there are spiritual creative energies (these are the Rays/Spirits) behind our world. With one lens, there is the material-scientific universe. With another lens of vision, there are these Rays/Spirits, which are like 'lights'. One of these lights shines through the physical centre, 'making' a man know/be himself as a physical being. Another light shines through the emotional centre, making a man know/be himself as an emotional being. And yet another light shines through the lower mental centre, making a man know/be himself as a thinker. At the first initiation, the throat or manas centre opens. The man would then be in a position to know/be himself as something more – something 'higher' than the ordinary thinking self …

6 The First Initiation

'The first three grades or degrees [of initiation] are concerned with study, with unceasing aspiration to grow spiritually and intellectually ... and also with living the life,' says Purucker.[1] Relating to the first three initiations, there is a dis-identificatory work the individual has to do – dis-identifying with the personal ego (which as a result, 'putrefies'); and a re-identificatory work the individual has to do – re-identifying with the soul (this is the Alchemist's 'whitening'). With respect to the former, the individual has to be able to say to himself: 'I have a body, but *I* am not my body; I have emotions, but *I* am not my emotions; I have a mind, but *I* am not my mind.' 'The travail of dis-identification is not necessarily tedious', writes Brunton, 'but equally it is not a hobby for idle hours.'[2] With respect to the re-identificatory work, the individual has to be able to say to himself: 'I, the soul, have physical, emotional and mental vehicles.'

The self is not the physical body, teaches Brunton, in his *The Quest of the Overself* (1937). If it was, then for one thing clairvoyance – where the self sees what *as a body* it couldn't – could not be. For another thing, being able (as some persons have demonstrated) to control one's heart rate – indeed to stop and start one's heart at will – could not be either. The fact that such things are, is proof that the life is not the body's, but the self's. The self is not the physical body; neither is it the emotional body, neither is it the mental body. All thoughts come to life *within* self-consciousness – this includes, of course, all thoughts on God, self, reality, etc. To study the self requires a singleness of attention, he says. To study other objects (ideas, the brain, etc.) is only evading this work. The limit of logical analysis is reached with this understanding of what the self is *not*. From here on the intellect can only be of use in *interpretation*, not in *research*. The present the self permanently resides in is a present *outside of time* (Character-time). This is because past, present, and future are thoughts which, like all thoughts, come to life within consciousness. The sequence of states of consciousness likewise is a sequence outside of time. Time is the product of the adult – thought-form building – mind (cf. Wilber's Mental stage and Gebser's perspectival worldview in Chapter 12).

FIGURE 6: THE FIRST THREE INITIATIONS

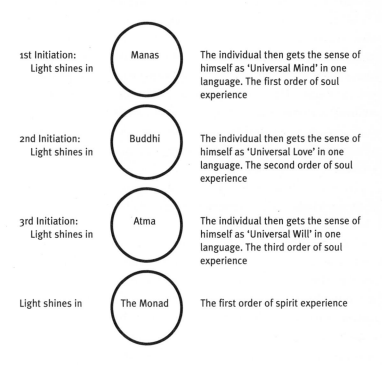

1st Initiation: Light shines in	Manas	The individual then gets the sense of himself as 'Universal Mind' in one language. The first order of soul experience
2nd Initiation: Light shines in	Buddhi	The individual then gets the sense of himself as 'Universal Love' in one language. The second order of soul experience
3rd Initiation: Light shines in	Atma	The individual then gets the sense of himself as 'Universal Will' in one language. The third order of soul experience
Light shines in	The Monad	The first order of spirit experience

At this stage (pre-first initiation) the dis-identificatory work involves particularly developing the quality of *dispassion*, says Barbara Domalske.[3] With respect to the second and third initiations it is *discrimination* and *detachment* respectively. The dispassion to be developed is towards the goals of ordinary life – material well-being, emotional happiness, and intellectual knowledge. There is nothing 'wrong' with any of these goals, but they do help maintain (and did in an earlier period help construct) the personal ego. Another word for dispassion is indifference, and Besant speaks of the need to cultivate a basic indifference to external things and affairs. This does not mean being emotionless, but it does refer to equanimity, and to distinguishing between that which no longer has any real worth in or to it (such as a personal hobby or possession), and that which has (which comes down to the pursuit and expression of the highest truth and being).

There is also the need for self-control in speech and action, she says. *Harmlessness* is the key word with respect to the former (not being obsequious, but being mindful of what one says, where it is coming from in the self, and its effects on others – that which serves to 'put up' the self, and 'put down' others, is harmful). And the latter particularly refers to control of the physical appetites. Clean living is preferred if it is not, at this stage at least, required. Some esotericists prescribe vegetarianism and abstaining from smoking and drinking alcohol, whilst others say this is 'between a man and his soul', with the understanding that in time the soul will let the man know – in a manner of speaking – what he can and can't do. Yet another need is to be able to quiet the mind through meditation, and a final need is for a tolerance that is 'the quiet acceptance of each man, each form of existence, as it is, without demand that it should be something other, shaped more to one's own liking.'[4] Rudolf Steiner also taught of the need for equanimity, the control of one's thoughts (through meditation) and actions, and the development of tolerance. He emphasized the need for developing the 'love of inner freedom', without which the lengthy gnostic project would not be sustained.[5] The 'deep intense longing for liberation' is, in fact, 'the promise of its own fulfilment', said Besant.[6]

The basic idea is this: As a child needs to give up his/her child consciousness in order to be an adult, so an individual has to give up his/her personal consciousness in order to be a 'spiritual adult'. At the same time as there is a dis-identificatory work to do, there is a re-identificatory work to do – the individual must 'build himself anew' as a spiritual being. This involves: a) visualization, or the individual picturing himself as a spiritual being (this particularly relates to this, the pre-first initiation stage); b) affirmation, or the individual telling himself he is this; and c) acting as that self. All in all, the individual must 'replace' the sense of himself as a person, with the sense of himself as a spiritual being here to serve life/God. He must replace his personal feeling nature with a/the spiritually loving nature, and his personal polarization around a spiritual doctrine with a genuinely 'above all that' polarization around the Wisdom that is. And – this refers particularly to the latter stages of the path – he must replace his personal will with the divine will. He must do what is best for the Whole, the Whole here being the planetary life that he has his first direct experience of at the third initiation. The key phrase in this last connection is: 'Not my will be done God, but yours'.

MEDITATION AND RAJA YOGA

> You should not have any mystical ideas about meditation, nor should you think it is easy. Meditation must be completely clear, in the modern sense. Patience and inner soul energy are needed, and, above all, it depends on an act that no one else can do for you: it requires an inner resolve that you stick to. When you begin to meditate, you are performing the only completely free activity there is in human life.
>
> Rudolf Steiner[7]

Union with the soul, Patanjali taught, is achieved through the subjugation of the mind as *chitta* – this would refer to *all* the 'stuff' that goes on in an individual's awareness (not just thoughts, but feelings, and sense-perceptions too). When this has been accomplished, the human being knows (or is in a position to know) himself as the soul. Two of the obstacles to union are: 1) lack of aspiration (Steiner's love of inner freedom as driving force); and 2) lack of intellectual development. A person can only 'get a handle' on the soul (and union with the soul does mean being the soul, *and* knowing one is the soul being) through metaphysical formulation, and as one's sense of self becomes more and more that of the soul, one's purview becomes more and more that of the soul, until it is completely that of the soul, and that purview can only be articulated metaphysically. Intellectual development is also required as we consider spiritual service especially in today's modern, developed world. Four other obstacles to union are: 3) 'wrong questioning' i.e. seeking answers from some outer authority or dogma; 4) an inability to concentrate on any given image or idea (more on this later); 5) 'laziness' i.e. just not putting the hours in to the gnostic project; and 6) a lack of dispassion towards material things (as covered). Muni says the aspirant must expiate his sins – chiefly lust (*kama*), anger (*krodha*), greed (*lobha*), and attachment (*moha*).[8] At any rate, as he sets out on the Path, he must have some manner of control over these things.

Removing the obstacles to union involves the practice of meditation, and also 'spiritual reading'. This does not refer to reading religious or esoteric literature (although this is regarded as complementary) but to developing, after stilling the mind, the intellectual intuition (to use Guénon's term), and thus revealing that which the ordinary discursive mind cannot reveal. Steiner refers to the 'Reading of the Hidden Script' in this connection.[9] There must also be devotion to *Ishvara*, taught Patanjali. This means devotion to both treading the Path and 'responding' to the divinity contacted in the form of 'living out' one's spirituality i.e. being a spiritual paragon in everyday life. Bailey set up a Raja Yoga school in 1923 called the *Arcane School*, and one of her books – *The Light of the Soul* (1927) – is a paraphrase of Patanjali's *Yoga Sutras*. Another of her books, *From Intellect to Intuition* (1932), describes in detail and in a less specialist language the stages of meditation that in some sense 'see the person through' the spiritual path (up to the fifth initiation at least). These stages she calls a) Concentration; b) Sustained Concentration; c) Contemplation; d) Illumination; and e) Inspiration. Max Heindel wrote of similar stages called Concentration, Meditation, Contemplation, Adoration, and Union. And Steiner's first three stages were called Imaginative Cognition, Inspiration, and Intuition. Steiner's fourth stage was that in which the pupil gained 'real knowledge of the relationship between Microcosm and Macrocosm',[10] and the fifth stage was that in which the union between man and the Divine – man and his initial God – was complete.

Bailey: Concentration

'In all schools of advanced or intellectual mysticism, the first and necessary step is the attainment of mind control', wrote Bailey[11]. When the average person closes his eyes, thoughts and feelings (and sensations – so learning how to physically relax is a requirement of meditation, and being in a quiet room whilst doing it is sensible) 'assault' him from every quarter. He tries to focus on one thought and finds others interrupting. The experience is like standing in the middle of a city, surrounded and at times overwhelmed by all the activity. For this reason the average person is 'turned off' meditation, feeling unable or unwilling to attempt to still the mind. Concentration is about fixing on something. What is proposed is that the student *fix on a divine self-image he newly creates for himself* – a 'new him' to which he can transfer, in some measure or manner, his identity.

Both the 'divine' and the 'self' parts make sense in the context of his aspiration. (What other type of image would have the power to capture and hold his attention to such a degree?) But there is also a crucial importance to the 'newly creates' part. There is something that this re-identificatory work – coupled with the dis-identificatory work spoken of – serves to precipitate. Bailey believed that this concentration activity can be adapted to, and must be adopted by, our educational systems (joining Eastern and Western cultures in an essential way), such that students are taught how to concentrate upon images which need not be traditionally 'religious', so long as they serve the same *function*. If humanity is collectively approaching the first initiation, we might wonder if our desire for a 're-enchantment of the world', and our widespread search for a new vision of reality that would include a divine human self-image, *is* precisely our collective dis-identificatory/re-identificatory effort.

Steiner: Imaginative Cognition

This is the first stage of higher cognition, says Steiner, following the one that 'depends upon sense-perception and upon the elaboration of sense-perception by an intellect that is bound to the senses ... [and which] may be called ... objective cognition'.[12] The pupil has to give himself up entirely to certain thought-pictures, the actual content of which is of little importance, *and yet* everything depends on the entire concentration of the soul upon one idea or thought-picture, placed, by an act of the will, in the very centre of consciousness. Dan Merkur, writing on the stages of ascension in Alexandrian Hermetism, says that for the would-be Hermetic initiate (the first initiate, this would be), the 'sense of self, which is ordinarily based in proprioception of the body, was to be distinguished intellectually from sensation of the body'.[13] 'Intellectually' is a tricky word here, but the basic idea remains the same: the man was to *know* 'I have a body, but *I* am not my body'.

In the visualization work there is a transfer of identity from the publicly and ordinarily held – which would be what materialism and the mirror tell the man he is – to the privately commissioned. Now, it is as if there is a higher cognition that is there all the while, trying to 'get through', but which is being *blocked* by ordinary cognition. This work serves in some measure to *un*block it. The purpose of the exercise, says Steiner, is to detach the soul from sense-perception. This detachment 'cannot be effected until man feels: Now I am forming a thought-picture by the use of forces that need no assistance from the senses or from the [intellect that is bound to the] brain'.[14]

The breakthrough in awareness has the effect of the individual then being able to say to himself:

> My consciousness is not extinguished when I abandon sense-perceptions and abandon also my ordinary intellectual thinking; I can lift myself right out of this thinking, and I then feel myself a living spiritual being, side by side with what I was before. Here then we have the first purely spiritual experience: the pupil becomes aware of himself as an I, an Ego, purely in the soul and spirit.[15]

BREAKTHROUGH

The breakthrough in awareness is *not* that the individual is the divine self-form that he has created. That would not be a breakthrough in awareness, merely auto-suggestion. Rather, the revelation is that he exists *not in this mental form or any other*, but as the creator of forms. Bailey says that the first initiation is a becoming aware of the *third* aspect of the soul, that of 'active intelligence' (we may read here 'creative consciousness'). With the second initiation it is a becoming aware of the second aspect of the soul, that of love. And with the third initiation it is a becoming aware of the first aspect of the soul, that of will.[16]

Steiner attempts to clarify: the student has to give himself up entirely to certain thought-pictures which, unlike thought-pictures that 'belong to everyday life', promote and enable a devoted concentration to them. The actual content is not the important thing; their usefulness in promoting and enabling this devoted concentration is. Each student will necessarily and ultimately settle upon (which is to say finally imagine in all its pictorial glory) his *own* symbol. His interpretation of what this symbol means will also ultimately be his own, and in the interpret*ing* of this comes about the initial self-transformation. There is no such self-transformation in the interpreting of other sorts of thought-pictures, because there the rational mind fixes upon forms derived from convention or dictation. Meditation means devoted concentration – an effort by the pupil *to infuse his life and meaning* into the symbol's. In this way, he refashions himself after it. His new identity is then one that embodies his highest aspirations and intuitions, having the full weight of his devotion and interpretive effort behind it. What the student achieves is the construct of himself, to himself, as a being that exists above and beyond the thought-pictures that belong to everyday life – he knows and sees himself as a/the soul.

The sceptic may say here that the student is simply brainwashing himself into believing what he is not, but the very ability to do what the student has done is testament to this ability being the self's. *Which goes to show that the self is other to the ordinary thought-pictures in which we posit its existence.* In other words, one person cannot say to another: 'This is what the self is, don't delude yourself', because his evidence lies in the ordinary thought-picture (and the rational argument that goes to sustain it) in itself. To the student who has mastered this first degree of esoteric training (the first initiate), he knows that his self is not to be 'found' in this thought-picture or that which others offer him (scientists, philosophers, theologians) – his is the self that has the ability to fashion its own form out of its own effort. To argue that the student's thought-picture is not a picture of his real self is ultimately only to preach doctrine, says Steiner. It is also for the evolution of the self to stop at the 'intellectual I' level. Later on, the student must drop this thought-picture, but by then it would have served its purpose; namely, to prove to the student that he was/is a thought-picture *builder* – the creator of forms. The soul can only know itself by positing itself through and in mind, and this is precisely what the student has done and therefore is at least connatural with. The argument as to whether or not the student was the soul (that there was one) before his 'invention' of one is annulled. The fact is, he is now what the soul would be anyway – therefore he is knowingly being the soul.

In Chapter 3 we spoke of seeing through the illusion of the physical plane, and Bailey refers to the 'Mystery of Matter' in connection with the first initiation.[17] *That* (the physical plane), is but a 'dream'. It is the content of the dreaming or the consciousness*ing*, of a dreamer or a consciousness*er*. The physical plane is *one* accordingly, and the consciousnesser can't be the individual self as a discrete objective being, because the knowledge of oneself as that has now been 'trumped'. The consciousnesser must then be 'everyone and no one'. What goes on, it seems, with respect to the first initiation, is five things:

1 The throat/manas centre opens.

2 Merkur uses the word 'proprioception', the usual meaning of which is 'the ability to sense the (physical) body'. This sense does not *go*, but knowing that this is 'mine' *does*. After the first initiation, the knowing-that-the-physical-body-is-mine is replaced by a knowing-that-this-is-a-vehicle-of-the-soul. It might be said that for the would-be *second* initiate (after the first initiation), the sense of self is *now* ordinarily based in proprioception of the *emotional* body. The man knows that his physical body isn't real, so he is 'thrown back' on the self-sense that developed at a later point in the development of his personality (which is as a feeler). Relatedly, he is thrown back on his/a belief-system that 'gives' man a more than material existence. 'The essence of the sublimation of the senses is their elevation into the region of *religion*', wrote Arthur Edward Waite,[18] and Steiner speaks of cognizing 'what lives inwardly, in our personality, also as an outer world'.[19] But later, man has to dis-identify with this body – the emotional plane is but a dream too.

3 The soul (or at least one order or aspect of it) is known.

4 There is a change of worldview from 'matter-based universe' to 'consciousness-based universe'.

5 Something which Theosophy calls the Causal Body, and esoteric Freemasonry the Temple of Solomon, has been partly built. After the *third* initiation, the ordinary proprioception of the individual is *here*, in this 'Temple'.

THE PURE CONSCIOUSNESS EVENT

The Pure Consciousness Event (PCE) is 'a condition of being entirely without any sensory or mental content', says Robert Forman.[20] One is in a state of unity with oneself, which, as the form of oneself cannot here be awarded to any objects of sensation or conception, means one is in a state of unity *with consciousness itself*. Forman equates this with the state of *Zazen* in Zen Buddhism. In Zazen one 'just sits', not attentive to any of the 'ten thousand things' which can occupy the mind, including all thoughts of Nirvana, becoming a Buddha, etc. 'I, though abiding in emptiness, am now abiding *in the fullness there of*', said Gadjin Nagao.[21] The PCE is occasional in the first instance, says Forman, but later becomes a permanent state of being side by side with the ordinary waking state. This second experience (considered in the next chapter) is the 'Dualistic Mystical State'.

In the PCE one's self-sense is not in this form or that. Objectively then, one no longer exists to oneself. Instead, one's self-identification is with consciousness itself, as the creative flow underlying sensory and mental content. The individual who has experienced a PCE *is* a first initiate then. He now knows himself as the soul (as the creative aspect of it at least), rather than as the body (the personality) – or rather as both, as Steiner ('I then feel myself a living spiritual being, side by side with what I was before') and Forman say. The two recognized strands of mysticism are the apophatic or 'emptying', and the kataphatic or 'imagistically filling'. The former we can see relates to the dis-identificatory work. There is a need to decrease 'the compulsive or intense cathexis of all of one's desires', such that 'one's attention is progressively available to sense its own quiet interior character', says Forman.[22] The kataphatic strand we can see relates to the re-identificatory work. The result of both is the breakthrough into that 'zone' in which thoughts are no longer, and thinker simply is. The kataphatic or re-identificatory work could be described as 'religious', but the PCE or first initiation experience is definitely a *trans*religious experience.

7 The Second and Third Initiations

THE SECOND INITIATION

Preceding Stages (development of personality):

Physical body sense

Emotional body sense

Lower mental body or I-sense

First Initiation:

Manas body or soul-as-creative-consciousness sense

I-sense as the physical body has now been trumped

The illusion of the physical plane seen through

The individual's new 'psychic centre of operations' level is the emotional

The first initiate has a new worldview, which he might express to others as 'creative consciousness is behind the universe'

Second Initiation:

Buddhi body or soul-as-love sense

I-sense as the emotional body has now been trumped

The illusion of the emotional plane seen through

The individual's new level is the lower mental

The second initiate has left religion behind

Third Initiation:

Atma body or soul-as-will sense; also Monad sense

I-sense as the lower mental body (I-sense per se) has now
been trumped

The illusion of the lower mental plane seen through

The individual's new level is the higher mental

The manas nature is by now well developed

The second stage of the work is about *consolidation*. The first initiate
knows himself as the soul, but because the emotional self is still
a 'power', he is not: a) as transpersonal and he can and now must
be; and b) as trans*religious* as he can and now must be. The dis-
identificatory work at this stage involves particularly developing the
quality of discrimination, says Domalske. That which must be
discriminated between is the real (the genuinely transcendent) and
the unreal (the merely referential). The emotional self is religious –
there would be, so long as this is still a power, an *attachment* to a
particular spiritual language. In a sense, the *second* initiate is a person
who has 'left religion behind'. The longest period to be found between
initiations, it is said, is between the first and second initiations. This

makes sense in consideration of the foregoing – not just the transreligious part, but the transpersonal part too.

The first initiate may have 'got over' himself as a physical being, but he must now get over himself as an emotional being. The 'Secret of the Sea' relates to the second initiation, says Bailey,[1] and the work here is one of breaking the illusion of 'the personal self, doubt and superstition', says Besant.[2] As earlier said, the individual must replace his personal feeling nature with a/the spiritually loving nature, and his personal polarization around a spiritual doctrine with a genuinely above all that polarization around the Wisdom that is. The second initiate *has,* so what now must *come,* is an established transpersonal (particularly transemotional), and transreligious aptitude. A higher faculty must be developed: the heart (buddhi) centre must be opened. The dis-identificatory work plus the re-identificatory work described here, serves to precipitate this opening. Zachary F Lansdowne says that after the first initiation, 'the emphasis is on using the illumined mind to discover, understand, and *dissipate the emotional.*'[3] And J S Bakula writes that if the first initiation 'marks the beginning of the end of the materialistic orientation to life', the second initiation 'marks the beginning of the end of emotional striving or the dominance of personal desire'.[4]

Bailey: Sustained Concentration / Steiner: Inspiration

The Sustained Concentration stage follows on from the Concentration stage, in that now more involved and complex 'seed-thoughts' can be used, says Bailey. Previously the individual built a divine self-image and projected himself into it. Now he is fixing on a seed-thought that affirms his soul-identity, and invoking his own soul. At the *Inspiration* stage, says Steiner, the pupil 'gives himself up entirely to the contemplation of his own activity of soul, which [earlier, and as he is realized] formed the picture'.[5] The consolidated or established soul-awareness is transemotional and transreligious, and Bailey taught that the first and second initiations are 'the only two initiations of significant importance at this time, owing to their *relative* immediacy'[6]. The work of the would-be second initiate is to clear away 'the storm aroused by his emotional nature, the dark clouds and mists in which he constantly walks and which he has created'.[7] The entire realm of the character's emotions and beliefs – *his everyday personal inner life* – has to be transcended (the astral/emotional plane is also the *belief-investment* plane[8]). The five things that seem to go on with respect to the second initiation are:

1 The heart/buddhi centre opens.
2 The ability to sense the emotional body does not go, but knowing that this is mine does. It is replaced by a knowing that this is a vehicle of the soul. The man now knows that his emotional body isn't real (the emotional plane is but a dream too), so he is thrown back on the personality self-sense that developed at a later point still (which is as a thinker). The man now 'lives' in his lower mental body.
3 The soul (as the love-wisdom nature) is known.
4 There is not so much a change of worldview again, as there is a change from an attachment to a language that expresses the Universal Mind-universe (which the first initiate knows is), to a 'position' that is beyond any such language.
5 The Causal Body has been further built.

THE DUALISTIC MYSTICAL STATE

The Dualistic Mystical State (DMS) is 'an experience of a permanent interior stillness, even while engaged in thought and activity – one remains aware of one's own awareness while simultaneously remaining conscious of thoughts, sensations and actions', says Forman.[9] The Dualistic Mystical State follows the period of occasional PCEs in a natural developmental sequence (and the achievement of the 'essential dualism of the mystic' was the aim of the *past* type of esoteric schools – the ones appended to the major religions, says Mary Bailey[10]). The result of living in the DMS state is 'acting rightly', for one's personal detachment permits the freer flow of the recognized spiritual qualities of compassion, understanding, and wisdom: in short, the 'heart' qualities.

The dis-identification work for the second initiation involves discriminating between the real and the unreal. Forman quotes Meister Eckhart as saying: 'When the detached heart has the highest aim, it must be towards the Nothing.'[11] We may equate the 'Nothing' here with the genuinely transpersonal/transreligious, and appreciate the *stable* Dualistic Mystical State as the achievement of the second initiate – he or she who has 'risen above' the emotional plane. (In *The Six Keys of Eudoxus*, the second Key of the work is the dissolution into the 'great sea of the Wise'.[12]) The DMS seems to evolve naturally into another state, says Forman, known as the 'peculiar oceanic feeling'. Here the sense of self 'seems to have become as if quasi-physically expanded, extending beyond the felt borders of the usual physical frame'.[13] This would relate in the esoteric understanding to the first experience the individual has of himself as the Monad or the *planetary life*.

THE THIRD INITIATION

There is a detachment to be developed by the individual from the personality *in toto*. The second initiate may have got over himself as an emotional being, but he has yet, and is now, to get over himself as a thinker – what we might call the Cartesian ('I am thinking, therefore I am') self. The new sense required is of being the soul with a complete personality vehicle for its creative-redemptive use. The previous stage saw the person *become* the soul in the seed-thought. There is a transition period between this stage and the next, wherein the need for seed-thoughts at all vanishes – the person then enters the *Contemplation* stage proper, says Bailey. The individual is definitely the soul, and not the personality, that is meditating now. The exercises *for* the third stage of *Intuition*, says Steiner, demand from the pupil that he 'disappear from consciousness not only the pictures to which he gave himself up in contemplation in order to arrive at Imaginative cognition, but also that own activity of soul, which he practised for the attainment of Inspiration'.[14]

'The next step [after the second initiation] is for the soul to take over the man's life from the personality', wrote Besant. The latter is the 'sum of inherited tendencies', whereas the soul is 'the growing "child of the sun", the future soul-man or Son of God'.[15] Bailey writes that the third initiate knows that 'the three worlds [physical, emotional, and lower mental] hold for him in the future naught, but only serve as a sphere for active service.'[16] Zachary Lansdowne speaks of the pre-third initiation period as being one of transcending the lower mind and becoming 'temporarily polarized in the realm of abstract thought, or the soul'.[17] Niels Bronsted says that at the third initiation, 'Man becomes a "journeyman" ... the soul takes control over the intellect and ... the entire personal standpoint is abandoned.'[18] And Arthur Edward Waite spoke of this stage as 'the mind's transfiguring'. He writes: 'In its highest development there is the consciousness already of that contact between the individual and the Universal Mind [here the planetary consciousness is meant] which is a foretaste of mystical union.'[19] The four things that seem to go on with respect to the third initiation are:

1 The forehead/atma centre opens. So too does the crown/Monad centre.

2 The ability to sense the lower mental body, the 'I', does not go, but knowing that this is mine does. It is replaced by a knowing that this is a vehicle of the soul. The *whole* personality is then a vehicle of the soul. The man knows that his I-body isn't real, so he is thrown back on the self-sense that he has built up all this while – here is the Causal Body. The man now 'lives' here.

3 The soul (as the will nature) is known, and so too is the spirit (as the third aspect of that). Vera Stanley Alder says that the third initiation sees the person change from being the mystic to the occultist. Directly relating to the Monad experience, she says: 'from this time forth the Initiate is an illumined man. *He knows.*'[20] C W Leadbeater writes that when the candidate has passed through the second initiation, 'he is ready for the third initiation, to become the *Anagamin*, which means literally "he who does not return,"

for it is expected of him that he will attain the next Initiation in the same incarnation.'[21] There is no return certainly from *knowing* what the disciple now knows. He continues: 'The Hindu name for this stage is the *Hamsa*, which means a swan, but the word is also considered to be a form of the sentence *So-ham*, "That am I". This would refer to the Monad experience – the experience the individual has of God looking out from behind his own eyes at Himself. Leadbeater also affirms that at the third initiation 'the causal body is especially developed. The ego [soul] is brought more closely into touch with the Monad, and is thus transfigured in very truth.'[22] It is said that science ends where philosophy begins, philosophy ends where mysticism begins, and mysticism ends where occultism begins. What was there before the Big Bang? Nothing, will say one person, because everything that was needed in order for there to have been a Big Bang was contained in the Big Bang. Of course, will say another person, because that's the way God made it. So, science ends where philosophy – what we choose to believe – begins. Philosophy ends where mysticism (mystical practice) begins, after it is conceded that the 'insect of the intellect simply cannot penetrate Reality', as Allan Combs expresses it.[23] And up until the third initiation, a man does not *know* his God. Thus, mysticism ends where occultism (where 'occult' refers to the supernatural, as in *of a higher kind of natural*) begins.

4 The Causal Body has been completely built (as in point 2).

The Causal Body is the alchemist's Philosopher's Stone and, changing the symbolism, if the alchemist started off with lead or salt, he would now have silver or mercury. When it comes to the third Key of Eudoxus, we read of *two* mercuries – white and red. The latter relates to the Spirit/Monad, which now 'enters the man from above'. To be clear, what we have now is the 'ordinary' soul, *plus* a Monad-impressed soul. Lead/salt/body, silver/mercury/soul, gold/sulphur/

spirit ... 'the appearance of the gold, which marks the beginning of the "red work", implies a direct intervention of a transcendent power', writes Maurice Aniane.[24] The appearance of the spirit opens up a whole new world, says Marsilio Ficino: 'When the stone shall have arrived at the first whiteness, there will be another world far more excellent than the former, where the *spirit* shall remain in the middle.'[25]

The Kabbalists' period of Nourishment has now ended (we recall the soul triad of Tiphereth, Geburah, and Chesed, which are coordinate with the Theosophist's Manas, Buddhi, and Atma). The journey so far has taken the Kabbalist out of the world of Assiah, and well and truly into the world of Yetzirah. Now the period of Maturity begins, and indeed the world of Briah (which is the next world of experience), is the world of the experience of the Elders of the House of Israel (the Lodge). The man now *knows*, says Alder, and so we may say that the Kabbalist can now enter that house and at least sit in the same room as the Elders. Man must (and will by now largely have) overcome his vegetable, animal, and egotistical natures, writes Halevi. The fruit of this work-to-date *is* that 'the man will be drawn up ... there to meet the descent of the Presence. In the utter silence and stillness ... he will face his unseen Maker.'[26]

THE UNITIVE MYSTICAL STATE

The Unitive Mystical State (UMS) is the sense of being unified with external reality, says Forman (the staring-us-in-the-face reality seen when the veil is lifted). In relating an experience by the German idealist Malwida von Meysenburg,[27] he says: 'It is as if the membranes of her experienced self became semi-permeable, and she flowed in, with or perhaps through her environment.'[28] Forman goes on to say how the experience of being of the same 'stuff' of the world can be of a transient or a permanent nature. In truth, we should only speak of a Unitive Mystical *State* in relation to the latter. In Theosophy, the Monad is first experienced at the third initiation. Bailey refers to this as being the experience of the *third* aspect of the Monad, with the second aspect being experienced at the fourth initiation, and the first aspect being experienced at the fifth initiation.[29] Full, i.e. permanent Monadic consciousness (the Unitive Mystical State proper) only is after five initiations then, just as full soul consciousness only is/was after three initiations.

8 The Fourth and Fifth Initiations

THE FOURTH INITIATION

> The initiatory journey leads 'far away from the beaten track of humans,' into what can sometimes seem unbearable darkness and isolation. But the journey eventually brings us back to exactly where we began. Nothing new is found that wasn't already present all along.

Peter Kingsley[1]

After a person has learnt to concentrate and thus be ready for sustained concentration, and sustained his concentration and thus learnt to transfer his identity to the soul, and contemplated and thus learnt to live as the soul, a new stage is reached. This is the stage of *Illumination*, says Bailey, where whatever yet remains of a personal ego must be and is now removed. It is the 'mystical crucifixion' stage. This – what seems like – the ultimate sacrifice made, the person is finally liberated. He now lives a life of divine inspiration (*Inspiration*: the final stage), where 'inspiration' means both to in-breathe (absorb through cognition) the one life, and out-breathe (in inspired thinking, feeling, and activity) the same one life. This is the goal for the evolution of the individual and of humanity, and from this point of attainment the whole business reveals itself to have been more metamorphic than educational, in that it is the soul and not the person which is now acknowledged to have been the subject that underwent the process.

> With the fourth initiation begins a new series of inner unfoldings – that is to say, not only are the study, the aspiration, and the living of the life, continued in the future stages, but with this degree something new occurs. From that moment the initiant starts to lose his personal humanity and to merge into divinity, i.e. there ensues the beginning of the loss of the merely human and the commencing of the entering into the divine state.
>
> G de Purucker[2]

The would-be fourth initiate must lay all, 'even his perfected personality [this refers to the third initiate], upon the altar of sacrifice, and stand bereft of all', says Bailey.[3] To understand this we must remind ourselves that Monadic consciousness is a *shared* consciousness. To *permanently* possess this consciousness requires dropping that most defining and resistant quality of the human condition: egocentricity. So long as this remains, even in a 'perfected personality', union cannot be achieved. The third initiate (and the nourished Kabbalist) would have broken the back of his ego, but that's not enough. The individual must go through a 'death' where, observes Jenny Wade, 'desire, attachment, and self-interest die as all egoism is extinguished.'[4] He can only following this death fully attain to the 'potential and true state of all human beings'.[5] To completely get over oneself requires the destruction also of the Causal Body, or the I-as-soul sense (the sense that can still generate pride, arrogance, etc.). 'The Fourth Initiation signifies the destruction of the causal body', affirms Bakula.[6]

> Let the Hands or the Head be at Labor, thy Heart ought nevertheless to rest in God. God is a Spirit; dwell in the Spirit, work in the Spirit, pray in the Spirit, and do every

Thing in the Spirit; for remember thou also art a Spirit, and thereby created in the Image of God. Therefore see that thy Desire attract not *Matter* unto thee, but as much as possible abstract thyself from all Matter whatever; and so, standing in the Center, present thyself as a vacant, naked Spirit before God, in Simplicity and Purity; and be sure thy Spirit draw in nothing but Spirit.

Jacob Boehme[7]

The fourth stage of the alchemical work, says Titus Burckhardt, is the 'new creation' (the Work of the Dawn) which, however, 'is not yet perfect, for the spiritual sun [the soul] ... is still attached to the cross of the elements [the Theosophists' fourfold lower man or Quaternary]'[8]. There is a need for what the yogi understands as *para vairagya* or 'absolute nonattachment'. Nonattachment, that is, to one's physical, emotional, and mental lives – this necessarily includes nonattachment to the individual's work in the world as a spiritual figure. We must 'get over ourselves' as *souls* – being sure, as Boehme says, that we draw in nothing but Spirit. 'Man's last and highest leave-taking is leaving God for God', wrote Meister Eckhart.[9] This is the true 'Dark Night of the Soul'. The I-as-soul sense must die, and this refers to the 'me' for instance in Jesus's words: 'My God, why hast thou forsaken me?' This nonattachment allows the greatest *attachment* to the buddhic or bliss-wisdom state.

The Dark Night of the Soul

In her classic work *Mysticism: A Study in the Nature and Development of Spiritual Consciousness* (1911), Evelyn Underhill says that when mystics are in the Dark Night of the Soul stage 'everything seems to "go wrong" with them. They are tormented by evil thoughts and abrupt temptations' – a general akrasia seems to come over them – and they 'lose grasp not only of their spiritual but also of their worldly affairs'. Furthermore: 'The health of those passing through this phase often suffers, they become "odd" and their friends forsake them; their intellectual life is at a low ebb. In their own words "trials of every kind," "exterior and interior crosses," abound.'[10] The world, it seems, finds these mystics repellent, and it is as if they are being completely broken down, humbled, so that they can be completely rebuilt along desired lines.

There are actually three deaths – or a three-in-one death – relating to the physical, emotional, and mental selves. The individual who lives most in the mental world (the world of thought) might find this death the hardest. Up until now the individual would have had a very rich and full 'spiritual intellectual' life, but now he is to reside principally on the buddhic level, which is as above the mental as that is above the emotional. It is also the case, relatedly, that the individual will suffer loneliness as the result of being on a completely different 'wavelength' now from most of his peers – the watershed of the third initiation, and certainly the subsequent accession to an otherworldly seat of knowledge, being a dividing line. Most individuals would probably find the emotional death the hardest though, as the buddhic nature is to replace the ordinary feeling nature as, well, the ordinary feeling nature. A 'finished article' is required in/of the person of the disciple. As previously said, and of particular note now, the disciple must replace his personal will with the divine will, so that his life in the world is as far as possible the beau idéal. All in all, the suffering the individual experiences (both internally, and reflected externally in the 'inimical atmosphere' that Underhill describes surrounding the mystic), is caused by the individual not being himself – the 'himself' here being pure soul beyond 'me-soul'.

In his book *The Soul and Its Destiny* (2004), John Nash speaks of the 'Hall of Learning' – this Hall we enter at, or maybe just before, the first initiation, and we remain students in this Hall until after the second initiation. Then we move up into the 'Hall of Wisdom', and our graduation from this is the final goal of Raja Yoga (the fifth initiation). Our time in the Hall of Wisdom includes the period between the third and the fourth initiations, and after the third initiation 'the soul then serves a kind of apprenticeship.'[11] We learn and are tested in our Hermetic Art, and 'if anything can prepare the individual for the renunciation of the lower nature at the fourth initiation, it is the many small renunciations made in the ordinary course of spiritual discipline.'[12] He makes clear, however, that the scale when it comes to the fourth initiation is very different.

'It might easily be imagined that exercises for spiritual training were something quite apart and had nothing whatever to do with moral development', writes Steiner.[13] But whereas it is true that spiritual training is not *ipso facto* moral training, without the work of moral purification there is danger to both the self and others. Lack of moral strength makes the conquest of self-conceit impossible, and this can grow so strong towards the end of the Path – bringing with it 'real experience of the Spirit' as it does[14] – as to be a force to contend with. Waite speaks of the fourth initiation as the great sacrifice – the 'complete immobilation of self and unreserved surrender into the hands of God'.[15] And Vera Stanley Alder, echoing all that has been said, says 'the fourth initiation can finally be attained only through complete sacrifice and the utmost suffering.'[16]

But it's not all pain – and Nash, as does Bailey, prefers to call the fourth initiation the *Renunciation*. That which is renounced or abandoned is – it becomes recognized – not what is most dear, but what is most inhibiting. 'Let us not imagine', says Purucker, 'that, because the words renunciation and sacrifice are often used, these imply the loss of anything of value. On the contrary, instead of a loss, it is an indescribable gain.'[17] To give up the things that belittle, that make one small, petty, and mean, 'is to cast away our fetters and take on freedom, the richness of the inner life and, above everything else, self-conscious recognition of one's essential unity with the All'.[18] Night eventually gives way to Dawn, sorrow is replaced by joy, an ineffable feeling that goes by the inadequate name 'compassion' bursts in on the awareness: After the fourth initiation, the person 'dwells ever on the plane of unity in his waking consciousness, on the buddhic plane', says Besant.[19] Here is peace abundant, and following the fourth initiation the individual 'ceases to make karma in the three worlds, but begins to work it off, or, literally, to "wind up his affairs"', says

Bailey.[20] The fourth initiation is the *establishment* of the occult awareness, and with this the individual can be in charge of large work and teaching many pupils, says Bailey.[21]

The first initiation is the experience of the first aspect of the soul (creative consciousness), or the birth in self-awareness of real soul-identity (as in the PCE). The second initiation is the experience of the second aspect of the soul (its quiddity, we might say, as transpersonal equanimity and transreligious wisdom), or the establishment in self-awareness of soul-identity (side by side with ordinary character awareness, as in the DMS). The third initiation is the experience of the third aspect of the soul, which has to do with the 'Will of the Father'. Also, there is the experience of the first aspect of 'Him' (as creative spirit), or the birth in self-awareness of real spirit-identity. The fourth initiation is the experience of the second aspect of God (*His* quiddity, we might say, which most religions are agreed is ultimate *Love*), or the establishment in self-awareness of spirit-identity. The fifth initiation (considered next) is the experience of the third aspect of God, which has to do with planetary purpose. There is a 'symmetry' to this initiatology that is worth reflecting upon:

Personal Development:	*From Personality to Soul:*
I am the one who senses (Physical Level)	I am not the one who senses
I am the one who feels (Emotional Level)	I am not the one who feels
I am the one who thinks (Lower Mental Level)	I am not the one who thinks

Initiations One to Three:	*Initiations Three to Five:*
First aspect of the soul	First aspect of the spirit
Second aspect of the soul	Second aspect of the spirit
Third aspect of the soul	Third aspect of the spirit

THE FIFTH INITIATION

[The fifth initiation] is the unification of the ego with the
Monad; and when that is achieved the man has attained the
object of his descent into matter – he has become the
Superman, or Adept. Now only, for the first time, does he
enter upon his real life, for the whole of this stupendous
process of evolution (through all the lower kingdoms and
then through the human kingdom up to the attainment of
Adeptship) is but a preparation for that true life of the
Spirit which begins only when man becomes more than
man.

C W Leadbeater[22]

The aim of initiation is to ally the human being with the
gods, which is begun by making the neophyte at one with his
own inner god. It means not only an alliance with the
divinities, but also that the initiant, the learner, if he succeed,
will pass behind veil after veil: first of the material universe,
and then of the other universes within the physical-material
one, each new passing behind a veil being the entering into a
grander mystery. Briefly, it is the self-conscious becoming-
at-one with the spiritual-divine universe; enlarging the
consciousness, so that from being merely human it takes
unto itself cosmic reaches ... In its higher stages, it brings
with it powers and an unfolding of the consciousness which
are verily godlike; but also does it imply the taking over
unto oneself of godlike responsibilities.

G de Purucker[23]

The fourth initiate is like a man who is emigrating, and who has gone
through all his doubts about (this refers to the path up to the third
initiation), and suffering at leaving and saying goodbye to others (this

refers to the fourth initiation), and is now looking ahead to settling in his new home – in Superbia, would say the Hermeticist. He has not yet arrived and settled though, whereas the fifth initiate *has*. The Kabbalist could previously enter the House and sit in the same room as the Elders – but probably just at a side table. Now he *is* an Elder. The Master in *The Supersensual Life* (employing the alchemical language of Boehme's day), writes that at the end of the Way: 'So shall thy light break forth as the morning; and after the redness thereof is passed, the Sun Himself, which thou waitest for, shall [fully] arise unto thee, and under His most healing wings thou shalt greatly rejoice; ascending and descending in His bright and salutiferous beams. Behold this is the true supersensual ground of life.'[24] The fifth initiate, in the Theosophical vocabulary, lives in his atmic body. 'At the fifth initiation he ascends ... on to the fifth [atmic] plane', writes Bailey,[25] as the fourth initiate lives in his buddhic body. In esoteric Freemasonry, he has become an 'entered apprentice' after the 'four initiations of the Threshold'. His concern with human and lower beings (and their evolution) is no longer 'personal' but, in a sense, *professional*. Says Bailey:

> Men are apt to think that the whole evolutionary process ... is merely a mode whereby men can reach perfection and develop better forms through which to manifest that perfection. But in the last analysis, human progress is purely relative and incidental. The factor of supreme importance is the ability of the planetary Logos to carry out His primary intention and bring His 'project' to a sound consummation, thus fulfilling the task given to Him by His great superior, the Solar Logos.[26]

There is one teaching chain, we are told, that is the historical passing of the Wisdom-baton: this would be the true 'apostolic' tradition. Then there is another teaching chain: fifth initiates, who are the Elect, and who work on behalf of a 'greater cause' (as above), teach fourth initiates. Fourth initiates, in their turn, and as almost-Adepts (almost, because as mere Arhats, they are still somewhat tied to the three worlds), teach third initiates. (In Modern Theosophy, fourth initiates are *Arhats*, and sixth initiates are *Chohans*.) Third initiates, who are people of vision, integrity, and wisdom – but who are yet susceptible to 'I-ness' (being apprentices still), teach lower initiates and non-initiates, i.e. all those who have yet to experience the Spirit for themselves, and therefore know beyond any doubt their oneness with God. Our purpose and destiny is to be self-conscious *of*, and through that focus of identity creatively and redemptively participate *in*, the life of that greater being in whom we live and move and have our being.

The Unitive Life

The fifth initiate possesses, in the Buddhist language, Nirvanic consciousness. To an extent this is a trans-earthly-concerns conscious-ness, but, says Besant: 'Has earth lost her child, is humanity bereft of her triumphant son? Nay! Now His face is turned to earth, His eyes beam with divinest compassion on the wandering sons of men ... He returns to earth to bless and guide humanity, Master of the Wisdom.'[27] And Underhill writes of the final mystical stage (the Unitive Life): 'As the law of our bodies is "earth to earth" so, strangely enough, is the law of our souls. The spirit of man having at last come to full consciousness of reality, completes the circle of Being; and returns to fertilize those levels of existence from which it sprang.'[28] The self is made part of the 'mystical Body of God' (referring to the body-consciousness of our Planetary Man), and is established as a 'power for life, a centre of energy, an actual parent of spiritual vitality in other men'.[29]

FIGURE 7: COMPARATIVE GNOSEOLOGY

Body/Soul/Spirit:
Hyle-Psyche-Pneuma (Gnosticism)
Circle-Line-Dot (Hermeticism)
Nefesh-Ruach-Neshamah (Kabbalism)
Personality-Soul-Monad (Modern Theosophy)
Salt/Lead-Mercury/Silver-Sulphur/Gold (Alchemy)

Seven Principles:
Moon-Mercury-Venus-The Sun-Mars-Jupiter-Saturn (archaic Mysteries)
Etheric-Emotional-Lower Mental-Higher Mental-Buddhic-Atmic-The Monad (Modern Theosophy)
Jesod-Hod-Netsah-Tiphereth-Geburah-Chesed-Binah (Kabbalism)

Unprincipled:
Earth (archaic Mysteries); Physical (Modern Theosophy); Malkulth (Kabbalism)

From Personality to Soul:
Initiations 1-3 and, in turn, Manasic, Buddhic and Atmic/The Monad centres opening (Modern Theosophy)
From Black to White or Work of the Night (Alchemy)
Period of Nourishment and from Assiah to Yetzirah (Kabbalism)
Concentration, Sustained Concentration and Contemplation stages (Bailey)
Imaginative Cognition, Inspiration and Intuition stages (Steiner)
Pure Consciousness Event, Dualistic Mystical State and Unitive Mystical Event (Forman)
Low Subtle, High Subtle and Low Causal stages (Wilber)

The above involves:
A dis-identificatory and a re-identificatory work (Modern Theosophy); a Putrefaction and a Whitening (Alchemy)

From Soul to Spirit:
Initiations 3-5 and relative enlightenment (Modern Theosophy)
From White to Red or Work of the Dawn (Alchemy)
Period of Maturity and from Yetzirah to Briah (Kabbalism)
Illumination and Inspiration stages (Bailey)
High Causal and Ultimate stages (Wilber)

After above:
Initiations 5-7+ (Modern Theosophy); From Red to Purple or Work of the Day (Alchemy); From Briah to Atziluth+ (Kabbalism)

The First Initiation:
New Birth (Boehme)
Awakening Consciousness (Kabbalism)

Period before this:
Probationary Path (Modern Theosophy); Gestation (Kabbalism); Purification (Alchemy)

The Way:	Path of Initiation (Modern Theosophy)
	Supersensual Way (Boehme)
	Work of the Chariot or Way of the Kabbalah (Kabbalism)
	Great Work (Gnosticism)
	True Philosophy (Neoplatonism)
	Royal Road, Hermetic Art or Solar Work (Alchemy)
The Soul Body (to build/make):	Causal Body (Modern Theosophy)
	Temple of Solomon (esoteric Freemasonry)
	Temple of Christ (Boehme)
	Seat of Solomon (Kabbalism)
	Philosopher's Stone (Alchemy)
Marriage 1:	Of man and Queen (Alchemy)
	Wedding of the Lamb (Boehme)
	Of Personality and Soul (Modern Theosophy).
Marriage 2:	Of Queen and King (Alchemy); of Soul and Spirit (Modern Theosophy)
Lower Man:	The Quaternary: Physical-Etheric-Emotional-Lower Mental (Modern Theosophy)
	Malkulth-Jesod-Hod-Netsah (Kabbalism)
Minus Unprincipled:	Etheric-Emotional-Lower Mental (Modern Theosophy); Jesod/Hod/Netsah (Kabbalism)
Higher Man:	The Ternary: Higher Mental-Buddhic-Atmic (Modern Theosophy)
	The Soul Triad: Tiphereth-Geburah-Chesed (Kabbalism)
The Eighth:	Ogdoad (archaic Mysteries)
	Sharing in the body-consciousness of our Solar Man after seven initiations (Modern Theosophy)
	The ostensible end of the Royal Road, leaving the Planetary for the Solar (Alchemy)
	Also relates to Chokmah (Kabbalism)
The Ninth:	Ennead (archaic Mysteries)
	After eight initiations (Modern Theosophy)
	Also relates to Kether (Kabbalism)
The Tenth:	Decad (archaic Mysteries)
	The Perfect Man after nine initiations (Modern Theosophy and Hermetic Occultism)
	Leaving the Solar for the Cosmic (Modern Theosophy and Alchemy)
	Also relates to Ain Soph (Kabbalism)

9 The Higher Initiations

THE SIXTH INITIATION

The fifth Key of the alchemical work (the work between the fourth and fifth initiations) is about perfecting 'our Paste', says *The Six Keys of Eudoxus*. It includes the 'Fermentation of the Stone … to make thereof the medicine of the Third order'.[1] The 'medicine' here is the radiating spirituality of the Adept. 'From now on the silent presence of the alchemist is a benediction on all beings. He is the secret king, the consciously central being who relates heaven and earth and ensures the good order of things', says Maurice Aniane.[2] Marsilio Ficino writes of the alchemist entering another life at a certain stage of the Work, *but*, we note, 'another life, where there will be *either* a perpetual day with those above, *or* a perpetual shade with those below'.[3] This relates to the sixth initiation, which Theosophists call the *Decision*.

'By the fifth initiation, the soul … has identified in consciousness with the monad', says John Nash; there now follows the 'Way of the Higher Evolution'.[4] This is a term he takes from Bailey, for whom the fifth initiation involves the revelation *of* a higher way (hence the name of this initiation: the Revelation). There is, of course, a wider cosmos beyond our planet. Alder speaks of the Adept choosing (having the right to choose) whether he takes the remaining two initiations within the seven manifested planes of our solar system. He may 'sacrifice himself to remain upon the earth to help with the progress of humanity', or, he may 'pass onwards to realms of development outside this planet, and even outside this solar system'.[5] Swami Rajarshi Muni also refers to this 'great decision'. If the liberated yogi so wishes, he or she can 'voluntarily leave his or her microcosmic sheaths and ascend to the highest heaven from which he or she need never return'.[6]

The sixth initiate is the Chohan – he or she who has discarded 'all the sheaths beneath the monadic vehicle, from the atmic to the physical', writes Bailey.[7] The sixth initiation is 'not compulsory as are the earlier five',[8] and the Chohan is a 'participant in *solar* and not merely planetary purposes'.[9] The sixth initiation is about making 'conscious contact with the Solar Logos'.[10] Would this refer to the first experience the individual has of sharing in the body-consciousness of our Solar Man, after the sharing in the body-consciousness of our Planetary Man? It appears so. With this, the Kabbalist moves from the world of Briah into the world of Atziluth.

Elsewhere in Theosophical literature we read of the 'seven paths' which a Master must choose from at the sixth initiation. Only one of these is serving our planetary life exclusively and completely, as a member of the Lodge. Leadbeater writes: 'of those who attain Adeptship comparatively few remain on our earth as members of the Occult Hierarchy.'[11] The existence of other paths can be appreciated as we consider the extra-planetary fields of consciousness – and therefore *arenas of work* – that open up after the fifth initiation. Leadbeater and Bailey write on the organization of this Lodge/ Hierarchy, the 'senior managers' of which are seventh (*Mahachohans*), eighth, or ninth initiates.

THE SEVENTH INITIATION

> The philosopher does not gaze at the stars through man-made telescopes alone, but by the transcendency of his internal faculties he is lifted up and taken into the very soul of the star itself ... The soul in him communes with the soul in his world, and both share in a common felicity.
>
> Manly Hall[12]

In the course of this great progress every man will some
day reach full consciousness on the highest of our planes,
the Divine plane, and be conscious simultaneously at all
levels of this Prakritic Cosmic plane, so that having in
Himself the power of the highest, He shall yet be able to
comprehend and function on the very lowest, and help
where help is needed. That omnipotence and omnipresence
surely await every one of us, and though this lower life may
not be worth living for anything that we may gain from it
for ourselves, yet it is magnificently worth enduring as a
necessary stage for the true life that lies before us.

C W Leadbeater[13]

At the seventh initiation, the individual 'enters into the Flame' and
'dominates the entire sphere of matter contained in the lowest cosmic
plane', writes Bailey.[14] The seventh initiate's vision begins to penetrate *beyond* the solar to see 'that which he has long realised to be a
basic theoretical fact, which is that our Solar Logos is involved in the
plans and purposes of a still greater Existence [our Parabrahman as
Cosmic Logos].'[15] Blavatsky wrote: 'The adepts have each their
Dhyani-Buddha, their elder "twin Soul," and they know it, calling it
"Father-Soul," and "Father-Fire." It is only at the last and supreme
initiation, however, that they learn it when placed face to face with the
bright "Image".'[16] This would be the 'solar spirit' above the 'planetary
spirit' of the Monad.

In the phraseology of ancient Egypt, successful initiation
conferred … the title 'Sons of the Sun'. Born into an even
brighter light, the resurrected man arose from the altar of
his spiritual travail transfigured with the solar glory.

W T S Thackara[17]

Man must return to the soul of the Sun and become like to it, wrote Agrippa. He also wrote: 'And when he hath received the light of the supreme degree, then his soul shall come to perfection, and be made like to the spirits of the Sun.'[18] Purucker affirms that the seventh initiate is the one who has finally winged his way back to the Sun, after dis-identifying with all his bodies (up to and including the Monad). 'Through initiation', he writes, 'if you pass successfully the tests, your spirit will wing its way from Earth through moon and planets on its way to the Sun.'[19] This last and supreme initiation 'comprises the meeting face to face with one's [ultimate] divine self, and the becoming-at-one with it'.[20] Dan Merkur refers to the last stage spoken of by A E Waite as a passing 'beyond the macrocosm to a union with the third person of the Christian Trinity'.[21] Our thoughts might return to the triangle in the Gnostic cosmos-picture here.

Commenting on the journey of Akiba ben Joseph, Z'ev ben Shimon Halevi writes: '[he] continued his ascension, so leaving the World of the Chariot [the planetary mesocosm] below.'[22] Akiba then entered that place which is 'sometimes perceived as clouds or a vast plain ... also seen as the vast surface of a cosmic sea'.[23] It is from this place of the Creator, 'that all created things emerge, descend, ascend and re-emerge. The Act of Creation occurs ... in the utterance of a word'.[24] It is the spiritual realization of this word (or Name) 'and its accompanying Divine state that Kabbalists seek while still incarnate, unless they wish to go beyond and so never return from a complete union with the Crown of Crowns'.[25]

BEYOND THE SEVENTH INITIATION

> Each step is marked, during its earlier course, by dropping
> something of the personal shackles and imperfections
> which keep us enchained in these realms of matter. We are
> told with reiterated insistence that the grandest rule of life is
> to foster within one's own being undying compassion for all
> that is, thus bringing about the winning of selflessness,
> which in turn enables the peregrinating monad ultimately

to become the Self of the cosmic spirit without loss to the monad of its individuality. In the above lies the secret of progress: to be greater one must become greater, to become greater one must abandon the less; *to encompass a solar system in one's understanding and life* one must give up, which means outgrow and surpass, the limits of the personality, of the mere human.

G de Purucker[26]

The seventh initiation is not, or perhaps need not be, the final initiation – the end of the Royal Road. Purucker recognizes ten initiations; Bailey and Leadbeater write of an eighth and a ninth initiation leading perhaps (in the language of the archaic Mysteries), from the Ogdoad to the Ennead, and then from the Ennead to the Empyrean. Eliphas Lévi wrote that the number nine was 'the hermit [who is Hermes] of the Tarot; *the number which refers to initiates*'.[27] The Empyrean is the 'Tenth' – the very same number claimed by the Kabbalists' Ain Soph. The seventh initiation brings us to share in the body-consciousness of our Solar Man. The eighth initiation would lead us to share (or begin to share) in a consciousness that extends beyond this: a trans-solar, or trans-*our* solar, or trans-our solar *body*, consciousness.

The development of the human being is but the passing from one state of consciousness to another … It is the progressing from consciousness polarised in the personality, lower self, or body, to that polarised in the higher self, ego, or soul, thence to a polarisation in the Monad, or Spirit, till the consciousness eventually is Divine. As the human being develops, the faculty of awareness extends first of all beyond the circumscribing walls that confine it within the lower kingdoms of nature (the mineral, vegetable and animal) to the three worlds of the evolving personality, to the planet whereon he plays his part, to the system wherein that planet revolves, *until it finally escapes from the solar system itself and becomes universal.*

Alice Bailey[28]

In Modern Theosophy, the eighth initiation is sometimes called the *Transition* (so there is a liminality here – up until now the individual was definitely confined to the seven manifested planes of our solar system), and the ninth initiation is called the *Refusal*. This last is 'a cosmic repetition of the Renunciation experience, this time devoid of the crucifixion aspect', says Bailey.[29] We note the word *cosmic* here: the individual at the ninth initiation 'refuses contact with the cosmic physical plane … unless he has chosen (at the sixth Initiation of Decision) the Path of World Service'.[30] Might this refer to a 'giving back' of a *cosmic* physical vehicle, so that a man now resides on the *cosmic emotional* plane? We recall that a Solar Man (in one of which we live and move and have our being) goes through initiations that relate to cosmic as opposed to solar planes. His first initiation would then be a seeing-through-the-illusion of the cosmic physical plane. After all, a Solar Man, in His own way, is just another 'Mr Baggins'. With the ninth initiation, 'the unit of consciousness is … perfect', says Bailey.[31] He, or it, is then the 'Perfect Man' (and *Ten* is his number) who, or which, 'passes on to work paralleling that of the Solar Logos'.[32] Beyond the seventh initiation is beyond our cosmos-system and into the world of Adam Kadmon perhaps, but we are to remember that we are still in the (albeit another kind of) natural world – the behind-the-veil, Aevertinal universe.

> And then, with all the [seven] energisings of the harmony
> stript from him, clothed in his proper Power, he cometh to
> that Nature which belongs unto the Eighth, and there with
> those-that-are hymneth the Father. They who are there
> welcome his coming there with joy; and he, made like to
> them that sojourn there, doth further hear the Powers who
> are above the Nature that belongs unto the Eighth, singing

their songs of praise to God in language of their own. And then they, in a band, go to the Father's home; of their own selves they make surrender of themselves to Powers, and [thus] becoming Powers they are in God. This is the good end for those who have gained Gnosis – to be made one with God. Why shouldst thou then delay? Must it not be, since thou hast all received, that thou shouldst to the worthy point the way, in order that through thee the race of mortal kind may by [thy] God be saved?

From *Poemandres*[33]

'It's Only Natural'

When we sit on a hilltop, say, and contemplate reality, *before* our minds 'kick in' and *tell us* what reality is (what we have experienced), *there*, right there, is the universe itself. We may feel part of a greater life and we are, and there is, exactly that, says esotericism. Bigger than man's body is the body of the Earth. Bigger than the Earth's body is the body of our sun/solar system. Bigger than our sun's body is the body of a larger cosmic 'object', and so on. Bigger than man's soul/consciousness and spirit *too*, says Theosophy (and also Traditionalism), is the soul and spirit of the Earth. And bigger than the Earth's soul and spirit is the soul and spirit of 'our' sun, and so on. Right here is Frithjof Schuon's total and real universe, populated by Manly Hall's degrees of awareness in space. Degrees of awareness that are at the same time Huston Smith's hierarchy of experiencing beings.

Treading the spiritual path is not a mad or a perverse pursuit, nor is it a 'religious' one per se, because it connects with Nature, with Cosmos, with Reality. 'Bear in mind that all the wisdom of the kabbalah deals with spiritual topics, which do not occupy time and space', wrote Yehuda Ashlag.[34] But 'time and space' here refers only to *Character*-time and space, which is real with a relative reality, but this relative reality has its being within and because of the absolute Reality. Which means spiritual topics are not, in the end, other to temporal topics, and although Reality is esoteric relative to ordinary (exoteric) experience, the Kabbalist/esotericist does not at any point leave what is either *normal* or *natural* (see 'The Challenge of the New Same Universe' in Chapter 13). A final word we will give to Purucker on the naturalness, experience, and result of treading the Path:

> Chelaship is nothing weird, nothing queer or erratic. If it were, it would not be chelaship. It is the most natural path for us to strive to follow, for by allying ourselves with the noblest within we are allying ourselves with the spiritual [also natural] forces which control and govern the universe. There is inspiration in the thought. The neophyte's life is a very beautiful one, and grows steadily more and more so as self-forgetfulness comes into the life in ever-larger degree. It is also a very sad one at times, and the sadness arises out of his inability to forget himself. He realizes that he is very, very lonely; that his heart is yearning for companionship. In other words, the human part of him longs to lean. But it is just the absence of these weaknesses that makes the master of life: the ability to stand alone, erect and strong in all circumstances. But never think that the mahatmas [adepts] are dried-up specimens of humanity, without human feelings or human sympathy. The contrary is the case. There is a far quicker life in them than in us, a far stronger and more pulsing vital flow; their sympathies are enlarged so greatly that we could not even understand them, although some day we shall. Their love encompasses all; they are impersonal and therefore are they becoming universal.[35]

PART THREE

CHANGING
WORLDVIEWS

10 Changing Worldviews

THE MODERN MENTALITY

> It is the tragedy of our time that the average individual
> learns too late that the materialistic concept of life has
> failed utterly in every department of living.

Manly Hall[1]

The modern mentality is no more than the product of a vast collective suggestion, said Guénon, writing in the first half of the 20th century. This suggestion is that this world of man and matter – what the 'ordinary character' sees – is the one reality. He might have therefore said the modern mentality of the general public, as distinct from the intelligentsia (the theologians, the philosophers – the latter group including the philosophers of nature or the scientific thinkers that history would see emerge). The general public, perhaps, tend to simply swallow whole, to then become their internal 'truth-picture', what the intelligentsia tell them. The history of ideas in the West over the last several centuries might be seen to be the history of the attempt by the intelligentsia to disentangle a cosmology and ontology from the mediaeval Christian (Traditional?) faith. There is this history, and concomitantly there is the history of the separation of Church and State and the taking over, by the latter, of the institution of the University and other social institutions.

The prevailing *paradigm* of Guénon's time – this word originally meaning 'pattern', but the term is now normally used to mean the prevailing intellectual view of things (in a discipline, or across disciplines, and here the latter is meant) – has been called by some, with a retrospective vision, the Cartesian-Newtonian paradigm. In the 17th century, the father of modern philosophy René Descartes's (1596-1650) analytical contemplation led him to a view of two things as undeniably real – a central human self as thinking subject (*res cogitans*), and a *res extensa* universe (or the world 'out there'). For Isaac Newton (1642-1727), this universe was constructed of solid atoms and was governed by what could now be called *natural* (without prefixing, or simply accepting as a synonym for this word, 'divine') laws. Their combined *new* universe, commonly accepted by a majority of thinkers, was such because apart from its esteemed objective existence (it was no longer a universe *in* God, although for the Churchgoing thinker it was still a universe *by* God), it was, says Richard Tarnas, 'understandable in exclusively physical and mathematical terms', and 'governed by regular natural laws'.[2]

Me here, World there – and God beyond both (perhaps)

A God could therefore be maintained who was the original Creator of the universe, but no longer was He necessarily still involved in it. And certainly no longer did we have to look 'upwards and inwards' for both *what* really existed and *how* this 'thing' worked – a thing which was now the *That* as opposed to the *This* which was ourselves. The human self henceforth became a philosophical problem – the 'mind-body' problem. Through analytical contemplation the self was not the Gnostic soul (the word *psyche* would no longer be widely used to mean anything 'higher' than the ordinary thinking subject), nor did it 'belong' to the objective universe, precisely because it was that thing's observer. Whilst philosophers continued to grapple with the mind-body problem (in accepting that this problem existed in the first place, these philosophers would not have been recognized as such by

95

their Neoplatonic predecessors), the practice of and belief in science grew. Belief, that is, in science possessing, or to possess in time, all the answers. Moreover, belief in the scientific *method* as the only method for establishing the truth.

As the 20th century progressed, this 'obvious reality' of man and matter, or mind and body, came to be challenged from *within* the Academy (never mind the esotericists who, in their divine-spark reality-view, largely found themselves operating *outside* of it). First of all, scientists discovered that atoms were not solid: that in fact, a base-line *substantial* component to the universe was hard to affirm. Secondly, the suspicion had been growing among philosophers since Descartes[3] (where it had not been present all along), that the mind as thinking subject was not simply the passive reflector of an external universe. A camera might capture what was out there 'in itself', but did the human mind? Instead, it came to be consensually and perhaps grudgingly accepted that the mind was active and creative in the process of perception and cognition. The question was: How much of *That* was what our minds 'gave' to it, and how much of *That* 'belonged' to it itself? Could it be that none of our knowledge of *That* contained elements that belonged to it itself, including its very *That*-ness?

Me here, World ... just in my mind?

THE POSTMODERN CONDITION

This question was not new, but what would emerge as a thought-worldwide, philosophically irrepressible, and *existentially felt* radical uncertainty of things was. Physics could no longer reassure us of one of the obvious two (matter/body). Then there was the 'discovery' of the unconscious and the division of the self (by Freud, for one, into id, ego, and superego). Added to this, cultural anthropologists and historians were now suggesting that our minds might be *entirely* the products of our as-a-whole societies and periods (*worldview* was the 'new' word). Also structuralists and other philosophers were telling us that all human thought takes place in language. There was no beyond-language reality or, if there was, we couldn't know it – we can never 'step out of' language to get the true reflection. Cultural-historical and conceptual-linguistic relativism then. From the Cartesian-Newtonian age of a fixed 'I' subject and a Nature object we were getting scientific knowledge of, we were now in the age of a psychological flux and an indeterminable reality, leaving us only with *dialogue* as the goal. The previous view (still dominant in the thought world outside of the humanities) was now 'naïve realism'.

Applied to the study of mysticism, the human-thought-cannot-escape-the-gravity-of-language conviction becomes the 'construct-ivist' view,[4] which is that what a mystic experiences is no more than the religious concepts and beliefs – his 'set of formularies' – he takes to the table of experience. That is to say, what he had previously internalized becomes (is projected outwards as) the 'God' he subsequently experiences in his 'spiritual' practice. But this trapped-in-language condition applies only to the discursive intellect, says esotericism (not to mention the *post hoc ergo propter hoc* fallacy in the claim that the religious context causes the content of mystical experience). The Divine Intellect, developed through gnosis, 'never works within the narrow confines of language', says Besant.[5] The constructivist convic-tion thus only reveals the 'underdevelopment' of the person who holds it. There is no getting away from the reality of and need for mystical practice. 'Are such practices the "other" of philosophy, feared and ridiculed because they challenge the only ground philosophy knows?' asked David Loy.[6]

The term *postmodernism* has been used to refer to a movement in art away from coherence, meaning, and 'art-ness'. It has also been used specifically to refer to a post-Modernist style of architecture. And provoking much debate, it has also been used to refer to a general intellectual mind-shift towards, some would say, nihilism, and certainly *pluralism*. The postmodernist in this last sense accepts 'the impossibility of apprehending an objective cosmic order with the [ordinary] human intelligence', says Richard Tarnas and, therefore, the 'pretence of any form of omniscience – philosophical, religious, scientific – must be abandoned'.[7] Huston Smith identifies a *minimal* postmodernism which contents itself with pointing out that we have no consensual worldview today; a *mainline* postmodernism which adds 'and never again will we have'; and a *hardcore* postmodernism which adds 'good riddance!', because these 'totalise' by 'marginalising' minority viewpoints.[8] Jean-Francoise Lyotard spoke of the post-modern *condition* as the 'legitimation crisis' caused by the 'collapse of metanarrative' – all we now see are the fictions or 'grand narratives' we told/tell ourselves. J J Clarke sees that there is *some kind* of postmodern paradigm today, that we may try and deny exists as a consensual worldview, but which is present *in* 'the rejection of grand narratives, of totalising worldviews, and absolute foundations'.[9]

This paradigm is *itself* a totalizing worldview though. So there is a big *philosophical* problem (there are just truth-claims, but this claim – that there are just truth-claims – is not just a truth-claim but is true), but also a *social* problem, with postmodernism or the postmodern condition. It leads to openness to the 'Other' (voice, person, culture, worldview), and therefore to the embrace of humanity. But because the self is no longer (to be) accepted as, in any fixed and final way, *meaningfully* related to other people (not to mention other creatures, life, God or Nature), it *permits* a social ideology of 'enlightened self-ishness'. And if we add a central identity to this list, it also *engenders* a mad consumerism. So the humanity embraced is not a *noble* (or even a necessarily *valuable*) humanity. Postmodernism stands up against intellectual totalitarianism, but does not, on the whole, stand up against the cultural totalitarianism of a dehumanizing materialism – nay, economism. The deconstructionist project is to reveal the 'ever-emptiness' of philosophy, and some see the entire Western tradition of thought as 'logocentric tyranny'. Daniel J Adams identifies the four defining characteristics of the postmodern age as: 1) the 'decline of the West' (we might also recognize a vilification of it); 2) Lyotard's legitimation crisis; 3) the 'intellectual marketplace' (with the economic rationalization of knowledge); and 4) deconstruction.[10]

From our 21st century perspective, it was not surprising then that a number of thinkers, for different reasons (existential angst, or simply ideologically), turned their attention geographically or historically elsewhere – outside the canonic West. Recent decades (in relation to the first type of reason chiefly, perhaps) have seen the emergence of new disciplines such as transpersonal psychology and Western Esotericism, both of which sit rather uncomfortably at the High Table of Academe. We have seen too the adoption by many Westerners of Eastern faiths and contemplative practices. And then there is the New Age subculture, movement or religion (qualifications vary), which might be seen to be the general public reflection *of* that new attention by a number of thinkers. In the next two chapters, we will look at the thought of three key figures in the train of spiritual-psychological thought that has served to put the soul, and some kind of perennial philosophy, back on the discussion table. To conclude this chapter, we will reflect on 'beyond the postmodern' and the idea of a (or to its proponents *the*) 'new paradigm'.

BEYOND THE POSTMODERN

Beyond the postmodern, for the postmodernist, would be the *acceptance* of the postmodern. For say what you will (he would say), language and culture shape experience and, to refer back to Alchemy, that head of the Black Dragon just can't be cut off. Well, without doing the alchemical work, it certainly cannot, replies the esotericist, and one cannot do that (the Great Work) at the same time as being a neutral philosophic observer of doing such. We now know, at least, says the postmodernist (claiming absoluteness), that there is no perennial philosophy. 'Is that so?', replies the esotericist. One can imagine a fishing conference, he might say, attended by a hundred fishing *theorists*, and a handful of *actual* fishermen. The subject for conference debate is: Is there a perennial fishing wisdom? The theorists conclude no – there are but different ideas on fishing. The actual fishermen just look at each other and smile. They know, because they *do* fishing (they don't just theorize about it), that there is a perennial fishing wisdom, but only the fact that there is can be truly communicated, never in itself the substance of it. But that should and does not prevent them from writing their own books on what the perennial fishing wisdom is. The perennial philosophy has to do with consciousness and spirit, says esotericism, and both of these will remain abstractions until experienced.

Analytical philosophy has brought forth some courageous responses to the postmodern condition, but the situation 'resembles nothing so much as a severe obsessive-compulsive sitting on his bed repeatedly tying and untying his shoes because he never quite gets it right', says Tarnas.[11] Kant recognized that what we see is what our reason sees or, as Tarnas expresses this revolution in Western thought that paved the way for postmodernism, 'Man's knowledge does not conform to objects, but objects conform to man's knowledge.'[12] But this simply means that the 'problem' is not located in nature/reality – only in our minds/psyches. *Before*, it came to be consensually accepted that the mind was active and creative in the process of perception and cognition. *Now* (and as a result), there appears to be a growing acceptance that we need to return to the practice of *real* philosophy which, as Jacob Needleman and David Appelbaum express it, is 'the art of living, which was once called wisdom'.[13]

J J Clarke's estimation of intercultural and interdisciplinary studies today is that it is in a 'hermeneutical' stage, following a comparativist stage in the late 19th and early 20th centuries, and a brief universalist/ perennialist stage (with the likes of Aldous Huxley and Frithjof Schuon) in the mid 20th century. He suggests that there is a wider and more serious 'new age religiosity' today than many would like to admit. With postmodernism there is an openness to the Other and to difference which, put the other way, means a willingness to let go of the self and the same. Of course for some people this is just 'the way things are': we have gone from mass oppression under Church authority, to mass liberation from Judaeo-Christian and indeed any ideological orthodoxy. Licence (and anomie) reigns. For a larger number though, the engagement in intercultural and interdisciplinary intercourse stems from *a more or less self-conscious desire for wider-than-self relations*. The spiritual journey starts with this desire – after one has had enough of floating in the pool of scepticism and relativism.

A new understanding, held by a new generation of thinkers, is that a paradigm is an intellectual view of things *that is the corollary of a state of awareness*. Where there is state of awareness A, there will be paradigm a; where there is state of awareness B, there will be paradigm b; and so on. The Cartesian-Newtonian, or more simply, *modern* paradigm (linking it with these two thinkers is somewhat arbitrary), is the corollary of the modern state of awareness. The postmodern paradigm (which a future historian might link with the names of a couple of postmodern philosophers, such as Jacques Derrida and Jean Baudrillard) is the corollary of the postmodern state of awareness. There would be 'minor' states of awareness and their paradigmatic corollaries between the modern and the post-modern. And there would be minor states of awareness and their paradigmatic corollaries between the postmodern and whatever major state came next.

THE NEW PARADIGM?

Traditionalists see in postmodernism, with its rejection of fixed principles and core values, the height of anti-Traditionalism. But at the same time they see a new Golden Age ahead. The first necessity for obtaining self-knowledge is to become profoundly conscious of ignorance, said Blavatsky, and we might reflect on the postmodern condition with respect to this. Man identifies first with the circle, then with the line of *consciousness*, say the Hermeticists, and we might reflect on a number of new onto/cosmogenetic models in 'new paradigm thought' here. Practising true philosophy is the way to go, say Needleman and Appelbaum – this involves meditation, or at least mystical practice of some sort, and we might reflect on the wider New Age religiosity here. Philosophy ends where mysticism begins, after it is realized that the discursive intellect simply can't penetrate reality, says esotericism. There is a dis-identificatory work to do (a putrefaction), and a re-identification work to do (a whitening). Bailey proposed that the student fix on a divine self-image he newly creates for himself (a new vision of reality that would include a divine self-image). Do we see humanity today doing this? The breakthrough in awareness, however, is not auto-suggestion – it is the Pure Consciousness Event (which a man, or humanity, would have to *rationalize* to himself/itself *in some language* – we might reflect specifically on the 'new physics' here).

The throat/manas/Tiphereth centre opens at the first initiation, says esotericism. There is a change of worldview from a matter-based universe to a consciousness-based universe, and do we see many philosophers of nature today affirming some such thing? The Causal Body/Seat of Solomon/Temple of Christ/Philosopher's Stone is then partly built. The individual's self-identification is with consciousness itself, as the creative flow underlying sensory and mental content. The Mystery of Matter has been discovered. Mr Baggins, after a 'modern' period of certainty, and a 'postmodern' period of no longer finding peace or truth anymore from/in any of his experiments/books, has seen through the illusion of the physical plane. *That*, is appreciated as just the content of the dreaming or the consciousnessing, of a collective dreamer or conciousnesser. Some of Mr Baggins's peers may simply *believe* in such, or hold as their *philosophy* a type of Transcendental Monism, but he (Mr Baggins) has *experienced* the Pure Consciousness Event/first initiation.

In his book *Global Mind Change: The Promise of the 21st Century* (1998), Willis Harman speaks of the new paradigm perspective which, recall, would be the corollary of a post-postmodern state of awareness. He uses a dream analogy to explain this new perspective. When we dream, he says, there is typically a 'story line' – events happen, and there seem to be causal relations (of *a* sort) between them. While we are dreaming, everything seems real enough, but when we awake we know that everything was but a dream, stemming from 'I, the dreamer'. The old paradigm (referring to the modern paradigm particularly, but also to the postmodern paradigm, seen as just the former stretching to breaking point), is a collective dreaming. Events happen, and there seem to be causal relations between them that we call 'scientific laws'. But new paradigmists (first initiates, it would seem) have awoken from this dream and know that it was but that, stemming from 'we, the dreamer'. Harman makes the connection between the old paradigm and the West's (representing modern man's) socio-economic policies and attitudes clear:

> Since modern society ascribes no 'reality' to inner experience, transcendent values have no power and materialistic values prevail. Thus it seems reasonable for society to be characterized by economic rationalization of an ever-increasing fraction of social behaviour and organization. Industrialization of production of goods and services gradually extends to more and more of human activities; increasingly, they all become included in the economy. One result is monetization and commercialization (all things coming to be measurable by and purchasable in units of currency). The economic rationalization of knowledge leads to the 'knowledge industry': to science justified by the technology it produces, and to education justified by the jobs it prepares for. Economic rationality becomes predominant in social and political decision-making, even when the decisions it leads to are unwise by other standards (such as the wellbeing of future generations). Technological solutions are attempted for problems that are basically socio-political in nature. The worth of persons (to say nothing of our nonhuman fellow creatures on earth) is assessed by their value in the economy. Humankind's relationship to the earth is essentially an exploitative one.[14]

These new paradigmists (if such there already are, or will be), it is important to remember, would be 'true' new paradigmists, not just new paradigm religionists or doctrinaires. We might alternatively call them *supra*modernists, on account of them: a) previously being post-modernists; and b) recognizing – from experiencing – the *supra*-conceptual. No matter how many philosophers deny the possibility of a Pure Consciousness Event, says Forman, it should be obvious that just because they, or us, have not experienced it (yet), doesn't mean that nobody has/can.[15] Esotericism reminds us here though that the new paradigm would be just the *next* paradigm along the line of consciousness, and there is also the Aevertinal to be 'reckoned with'. The latter may not be fully appreciated until at or just before the third initiation (when the Work of the Night has been completed). But, if it is the case that we need *today*, as a civilization, *a* new map to continue with, why be satisfied with just the atlas page that shows our starting point and our *first* stopping point, when we can have the whole atlas? At the same time, the first and last teaching of esotericism is 'man, know thyself': we are not to 'know' through other people's gnosis, and that includes the group of esotericists as a whole.

11 Spiritual Psychology I: Carl Jung and Roberto Assagioli

It is precisely the god-like in ourselves that we are ambivalent about, fascinated by and fearful of, motivated to and defensive against.

Abraham Maslow[1]

The word psychology means law or science of the self. But what is the self? It stands to reason that the psychological school one accepts depends upon the self one accepts – through analytical contemplation or identity experience. The two dominant schools or 'forces' in psychology, at least until recent decades, were the behaviourist and the psychoanalytic (with the work of, particularly, John B Watson and Sigmund Freud respectively). The behaviourists study empirically measurable behaviour, and it might be said that the understanding of the self here is as an animal – the social animal, man. Psychoanalysts study the inner world of thoughts and feelings of this same man, and a personal unconscious formed in childhood. Their understanding of the self is as a character or personality. These schools came under attack for, with respect to the first, ignoring 'our everyday mind, our very real, immediate awareness of being', says John Welwood.[2] And with respect to the second, for ignoring 'large areas of human mental life, especially those connected with religious experience and expanded states of consciousness', says J J Clarke.[3]

In the 1950s, a new school – humanistic – championed by Abraham Maslow for one, understood the self as an individual with a 'hierarchy of needs', the highest of which was an existential-psychological need for 'self-actualization'. The utmost form of this could be a *divine* self-actualization. Maslow anticipated fourth and *fifth* forces/schools, which he labelled 'transpersonal' and 'transhuman', says Douglas Russell.[4] The possibility of a fifth school based on a 'theosophical world-view' was raised in an article by Dane Rudhyar,[5] and for J S Bakula,[6] the transhumanistic refers to the path of initiation leading, as we have seen, to the body-consciousness, first, of our Planetary Man as God. A trans*personal* school did emerge in the 1970s, and here the understanding of the ultimate self is as a Pure Consciousness of some kind.

Roger Walsh and Francis Vaughan speak of transpersonal psychology as the study of 'the nature, varieties, causes, and effects of transpersonal experiences and development, as well as the psychologies, philosophies, disciplines, arts, cultures, lifestyles, reactions, and religions that are inspired by them, or that seek to induce, express, apply, or understand them'.[7] Michael Daniels makes clear that 'because the transpersonal involves much more than the phenomena of religion, transpersonal psychology is not the same as the *psychology of religion*.'[8] Transpersonal psychology offers a 'contextualization' of non-transpersonal psychology, and an experimental-empirical wing looks at 'Altered States of Consciousness', whilst a theoretical wing proffers 'maps of consciousness' drawing upon Western, but chiefly Eastern mystical schools of thought (together with descriptions of higher states of awareness by mystics). There is transpersonal *psychology* (and psychotherapy), and then there is a transpersonal *perspective* applied to other fields e.g. sociology, education, and governance. In this chapter, we will look at two major transpersonal psychologists – Carl Jung and Roberto Assagioli – and in the next chapter a third, Ken Wilber, whose thoughts straddle the second, third, and fourth schools.

CARL JUNG

> Despite the materialistic tendency to understand the psyche as a mere reflection or imprint of physical and chemical processes, there is not a single proof of this hypothesis … There is thus no ground at all for regarding the psyche as something secondary or as an epiphenomenon.
>
> Carl Jung[9]

Splitting with his former mentor Freud for, as he saw it, seeing or considering only the 'animal man', Carl Jung (1875-1961) is, says William Bloom, the psychologist most referred to in the holistic world.[10] By 'holistic world', Bloom refers to a contemporary community of thinkers and New Ageists who broadly share a more-than-man-and-matter perspective or belief, and who generally conceive the emergence of a new holistic consciousness. Jung was passionately interested in what some today call 'alternative spiritualities'. He was particularly knowledgeable on Gnosticism and Alchemy, and had a fascination for Theosophy and Anthroposophy which he saw as 'pure Gnosticism in a Hindu dress'.[11] He was also a student of Eastern religions and an authority on world mythology. Like Maslow, his chief concern was with self-actualization or 'self-realization'. William Quinn sees Jung as sympathetic to Traditionalism in recognizing a Western cultural descent of sorts (since the Middle Ages), with modern Christianity lacking a 'psychological culture'. Heathenism is to be expected when the Church only provides for a meeting with Christ 'from without', rather than 'from within' as an *Archetype* of the Self (see below). Other thinkers such as Gerhard Wehr have described Jung as an 'esoteric Christian' in this connection.[12]

Jung saw the Gnostics as the 'spiritual ancestors of his own teachings', says Stephan Hoeller,[13] and believed that the historical passage of these teachings was through the mediaeval and Renaissance Alchemists, whose philosopher's stone-goal was spiritual self-realization (as the soul at least). Jung felt humans to be naturally religious – naturally *spiritual* might be a better term to use – with the modern mentality being polarized around an illness-producing, 'Mythless' axis. 'About a third of my cases', he wrote, 'are suffering from no clinically definable neurosis, but from the senselessness and emptiness of their lives. It seems to me ... that this can be described as the general neurosis of our time.'[14] What was the cure (or at least the beginning of a cure) for this? 'Individual self-reflection, return of the individual to the ground of human nature ... here is the beginning of a cure for that blindness that reigns at the present hour.'[15] Jung's mainstream analytical psychology features two basic personality types (extrovert and introvert), and four basic faculties of psychological operation (thinking, feeling, sensation, and intuition). It features too a *collective* unconscious.

In Jung's view there are not just the daily, personal 'residues' in the unconscious mind, but archaic ones, harking back to forgotten mythologies. Here were archetypes such as the Persona, which was the self we present to the outside world, and the Shadow, which approximates the Freudian unconscious, at least in being 'below' the mature intelligent centre of the psyche. Other archetypes included the Anima and the Animus, the Mother, the Father, the Hero, the Wise Old Man, the Trickster, and the Hermaphrodite. In human cultural productions cross-culturally and cross-historically, we see the same *psychically resonating* symbols of the likes of these. There was/is thus a common psychological basis underlying the ancient symbol systems of different cultures. For Jung the mystic, the goal of becoming a conscious and fully-realized person 'unites the most diverse cultures in a common task',[16] and ultimately this was a person *in God*.

The first half of the person's life (0 to 40 years perhaps), Jung depicted as the sun climbing to the meridian, and in this period one established oneself in the world (on the way, often repressing one's Shadow nature). The second half of the person's life he depicted as the sun completing its curve, and in this period one proceeded – or should proceed – to 'go beyond oneself' or, in other languages, to practice the Tao or the Way. On this 'individuation' journey (the *Principium Individuationis*), one needs to deal with the Shadow part of oneself, and one truly meets and 'lives' the archetypes, in the sense that *the full human-spiritual experience* is a 'negotiation' with these. 'Between them', Jung wrote, 'the patient iron is forged into an indestructible whole, an "individual."'[17] The end of the journey is a union with one's highest (divine) self. Here we have the archetype of the Self, symbolized, for example, by Christ. A 'normal' (Traditional?) culture would be one where such archetypes were in its Myth (worldview), and there would thus be a harmonious and stable individual-culture-life 'psychological' relationship. Jung's psychology was 'essentially the psychology of relationship', says Bakula.[18]

The title of Jung's last major work was the *Mysterium Coniunctionis* (1955) – a work on the alchemical Great Work. This Work was, for Jung, the 'unpopular, ambiguous and dangerous … voyage of discovery to the other pole of the world'.[19] Jung did not believe that Westerners needed to look eastwards for spiritual models and practices – a 'Western Yoga' was realizable from the Western Tradition. Today, Jung *is* perhaps the psychologist most referred to in the holistic world, because his thoughts and concerns encompass such subjects as the 'higher self' (the soul, if not the spirit), gnosis, the re-esotericization of Christianity, and the wider respiritualization of Western culture. Jung was not an esotericist, but his view on the ultimate self of man appears to reach toward, if it did not intimate, a fifth school (theosophical, transhuman) perspective:

> Man is a gateway, through which one enters from the outer
> world of the gods, demons and souls, into the inner world,

from the greater world into the smaller world. Small and insignificant is man; one leaves him soon behind, and once again one finds oneself in infinite space, in the smaller or innermost infinity. In immeasurable distance there glimmers a solitary star in the zenith. This is the one God of this one man. This is his world, his Pleroma, his divinity. In this world, man is Abraxas, who gives birth to or devours his own world. *This star is man's God and goal.*[20]

A DIGRESSION

We might digress at this point and consider the modern scientific universe and the archaic Mysteries. The modern scientific paradigm was the Newtonian – we can drop the prefixing 'Cartesian-', appropriate for the modern across-disciplines (general) paradigm, and replace it with the more particular 'Copernican-'. The Copernican part was the revolution that saw the earth as the centre of the universe (with the moon, the sun, and the planets revolving around it), replaced with the sun as the centre of the universe. Actually, the sun not as the centre of the *universe*, but merely of our solar system. The previous picture saw the stars *not* as stretching out to various distances in space; the stars instead bespeckled a firmamental 'shell'. The previous picture was geocentric; the new picture was heliocentric, with the sun as *a* star around which the earth as *a* planet – not necessarily special in any way – revolved. Traditionalists see Western culture (before the likes of Copernicus, Descartes, and Newton) as Traditional in at least having a Great Chain of Being worldview. This was a time before there was an 'independent' intelligentsia.

In the archaic Mysteries we see a celestial-body earth *representing* man's (apparently objective) material body, and a celestial-body septenary (the moon, the sun, and the five planets) representing spiritual-esoteric *principles*. The latter are 'above' the former. The true philosopher would therefore see *some sort of truth* in the pre-Copernican universe-picture, relating to *our* cosmos-system at least. The new philosophy of Descartes did away with Maya, or everything being relatively real, remember Blavatsky, 'for the cogniser is also a reflection, and the things cognised are therefore as real to him as himself.' With Copernicus, a *relative* geocentric truth was also done away with. The new universe-picture (today's esotericist would say) was yet progressive though, because it opened to hope an 'all cosmos-systems, all logoic-levels'[21] understanding. If the ideal society depends upon the dissemination and general acceptance of *a form of* the perennial philosophy, then such a form today *could* accommodate both the 'horizontal' modern scientific universe, *and* the 'vertical' pre-modern (pre-scientific and pre-independent intelligentsia) universe.

ROBERTO ASSAGIOLI

'There comes a time', Aldous Huxley wrote, 'when one asks even of Shakespeare, even of Beethoven, is this all?'[22] What is the goal or limit of personal development? Is it the mastery of the nature such that one is freed from the control of childhood habits, adolescent feelings, and cultural ideas? One would then be a free thinker and a mature individual, and perhaps enjoy much of the same view as Shakespeare and Beethoven, but would one have realized one's *ultimate* potential? ('Is this all?') That, mystics and esotericists tell us, is to unite in consciousness with God. Beyond *personal* development lies *spiritual* development then, and this was the view of both Jung and the Italian psychiatrist Roberto Assagioli. The latter's school of *Psychosynthesis*, developed over many decades since a system was first sketched out in a doctoral thesis in 1910, addresses personal and spiritual development and therapy. 'In its methods, Psychosynthesis combines techniques of psychotherapy, education and spiritual discipline', says Douglas Russell.[23] Psychosynthesis is a conception of psychological life, a method of psychological development, a philosophy and method of treatment for psychological and psychosomatic disturbances, *and* a philosophy and method of integral (personal and spiritual) education.

Assagioli's model of the psyche features a divine unconscious, and a soul identity as distinct from a personality identity. His system features a *Lower Unconscious* as the home of 'those elementary psychological activities which direct the life of the body'.[24] This is the 'child mind', which is susceptible to such diseases as phobias, obsessions, and compulsive urges. The *Middle Unconscious* was the 'adolescent mind', susceptible to such diseases as – to use a modern term – 'script pathologies' such as racism. The *Higher Unconscious* was the 'higher mind'. It is the home of the 'higher feelings, such as altruistic love; of genius and of the states of contemplation, illumination and ecstasy'.[25] The *Field of Consciousness* was the incessant flow of sensations, images, desires, thoughts, etc. in the 'adult mind', not to be confused with that per se as the *Conscious Self*. In most individuals, said Assagioli, this adult mind was little developed. Most of us are instead controlled by our adolescent minds, or else 'drift on the surface of the mind-stream' [the field of consciousness].[26] The establishment of the Conscious Self is thus the first work of Psychosynthesis. The *Higher Self* was the spiritual/transpersonal self in the individual whose 'projection in the field of the personality' was the Conscious Self. Finally, as said, there was the one ultimate divine unconscious.

The first work Psychosynthesis recognizes is the establishment of the Conscious Self. This *may* involve psychoanalysis (to deal with problems picked up on the path of personal development generally; diseases in the lower unconscious particularly), but Psychosynthesis has a broader *educational* agenda in its goal of outing mature conscious selves. Society needs such, we as individuals need such too – we need to be controlled not by our child or adolescent minds, but by a centre from which we may act freely, intelligently, and maturely. Assagioli distinguished between *personal* Psychosynthesis and *spiritual* Psychosynthesis. Personal Psychosynthesis may involve psychoanalysis, but as the higher goal on the therapist's mind is personal development, he brings the patient into the psychoanalytic work at the earliest opportunity. This is much as a teacher brings his pupil into the work of solving mathematical problems when he is old enough. This bringing-in is a forcing-out of the pupil's *own* mathematical mind. Here the patient's own psychoanalytic mind is being forced out – the same type of mind as the Psychosynthesis therapist, who is a mature conscious self.

Where a Psychosynthesis therapist is also united in consciousness with his higher self, he can now be a spiritual Psychosynthesis therapist. His higher goal now – working with a patient who is at least to some extent already a mature conscious self – is spiritual development. Just as the work of personal Psychosynthesis may involve psychoanalysis, so the work of spiritual Psychosynthesis may involve dealing with problems picked up on the path of spiritual development. Problems *preceding* spiritual awakening – which are caused by the ever coming closer of the spiritual awareness – include intellectual doubt and emotional depression. This inner dis-ease, familiar to many a postmodern philosopher today perhaps, may manifest in, for example, nervous tension and insomnia, and be misdiagnosed by the ordinary psychologist as psychoneurosis or even schizophrenia.

Problems *following* spiritual awakening include: a) the 'mountains and valleys' condition characteristic of the Christian mystic, which resembles a condition of manic depression, and which is linked to the cyclical nature of spiritual impression; b) an overcritical attitude towards oneself (one's yet-imperfect being) resulting in a paralytic state in terms of creative spiritual living; and c) problems caused by the individual still being pre-mature (that is, lacking in intelligent understanding and self-control) in certain important areas. As a result he may think that he is hearing voices, for example, or think that he, as his *persona*, is God. Another problem, which John Welwood pellucidly describes, is 'spiritual bypassing'.[27] This is where an individual does not let the soul take charge of his social animal-life: he keeps his spirituality 'in the head'.

Assagioli makes the point that there is a need to distinguish clearly between problems picked up on the path of personal development – which both personal Psychosynthesis and the ordinary psychologist recognize and deal with, and problems picked up on the path of spiritual development. Treating a patient with a 'spiritual problem' with a treatment for a personal problem, may actually make things worse – after all, it is not psychological alignment with man-and-matter 'reality' that we are after with the spiritual patient. The spiritual Psychosynthesis therapist brings the patient into the work of solving spiritual problems, again at the earliest opportunity. These *are* all dealt with by throwing the light of the higher mind upon them, and this is therefore the one to be forced out. Assagioli used and encouraged the techniques and practice of Raja Yoga in this respect. In both personal and spiritual Psychosynthesis the therapist works, necessarily, with the patient's own *will* – the will to heal, and the will to evolve or to achieve integration. Ken Wilber, who we will consider next, recognizes the will as *Eros* – the force of life and integration. There is also *Thanatos*, the force of death and disintegration. Eros or the force of will is worked with by the Psychosynthesis therapist in *development* per se, and Thanatos is worked with in *therapy* per se.

12 Spiritual Psychology II: Ken Wilber

Ken Wilber is a contemporary psychologist and popular philosopher whose 'full spectrum' model of the human psyche we will consider here. Frank Visser believes that the relationship between transpersonal psychological models and understandings, such as Wilber's, and esoteric models and understandings, such as Theosophy's, have yet to be fully explored.[1] We will precipitate this by referring to Theosophy's initiatology in this section. The reader is also referred to an article by Robert P Turner in this connection.[2] Wilber's psychology begins with the Atman as a Pure Consciousness (it is Atman with respect to being the highest component of the individual's psyche, otherwise it is Brahman/God). To experience the Atman would be an experience in which God (or some such Whole) looks out from behind the individual's eyes at Himself (again, as some such Whole). The individual is not 'excluded' here: he is a participant in the experience.

At the end of evolution in the Theosophical scheme, man participates in the body-consciousness of our Solar Man, but prior to this there is a participation in the body-consciousness of our Planetary

Man. This latter relates to the Monad. What Wilber calls Brahman, would say the Theosophist, is a Whole, but it is not the Whole that is the body-consciousness of our Solar Man. His scheme stops, as it were, at the 2nd solar plane. Turner writes: 'Recognising that the fifth initiation represents perfection from the perspective of human existence ... it is understandable that Wilber's spectrum – and teachings from other spiritual traditions – culminate as they do on the monadic plane.'[3] But esoteric psychology, he says, 'addresses consciousness development beyond the level of [this] ultimate Unity'.[4]

Man finds himself in the manifestation, say the Gnostics. This man sees a real world, which is to say a real physical-material world, which he is part of. See through the illusion of a physical self, and obviously one can no longer accept a physical universe, only a universe which is the content of 'we the dreamer'. This is the reality-perspective of the first initiate. This is the *Low Subtle* stage of consciousness evolution, *might* agree Wilber. In his book *The Atman Project* (1980), Wilber lists several stages of evolution after, if we like, the 'ordinary character' consciousness. As this is the consciousness of the *adult* individual, he precedes these with stages of consciousness from birth up to this (hence full spectrum).

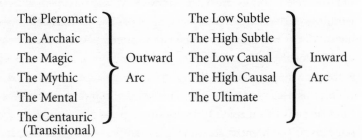

The Pleromatic		The Low Subtle	
The Archaic		The High Subtle	
The Magic	Outward	The Low Causal	Inward
The Mythic	Arc	The High Causal	Arc
The Mental		The Ultimate	
The Centauric (Transitional)			

THE OUTWARD ARC

The stages are as listed above, taken from the aforementioned book. With Assagioli, we have the idea of the lower unconscious as the child mind, the middle unconscious as the adolescent mind, and the conscious self as the adult mind. In Theosophy, we have the idea of personal development as the 'appropriation', and then a 'polarization' there, in turn, of the physical, emotional and mental bodies (as the lower centres open one by one). We learn to act and, for a while, physical sensations are everything. Then we learn to feel and imagine, and for a while – referring to older children and adolescents – we are polarized in our emotional and imaginative lives. Next we learn to think and are rational creatures – we have moved on (now referring to the ordinary unconscious) from our juvenile natures. With Wilber, we have 'structures' of consciousness which change as we grow up. With the Mental stage/structure, reality is 'arranged' into the universe of three spatial dimensions and a linear time, with the self as an object in this, that the ordinary adult sees. Wilber sees the stages playing out not just in the life of the individual, but historically as psychological Ages of Man. Assagioli held a similar view of human history as revealing a growing-up of man from a child to an adult mind.

Wilber's work draws upon the work – with respect to the Outward Arc stages – of psychologists such as Jean Piaget and Erich Neumann and, of particular note, cultural historian Jean Gebser. Pleromatic[5] period men and babies did/do not really experience the world, and as such had/have no real awareness of themselves as distinct from nature. Archaic[6] period men and infants experienced/experience the world through their bodies (there is a growing physical self-sense here). Magic[7] period men and children experienced/experience the world through their emotions (there is a firm physical self-sense here, and a growing emotional self-sense). Mythic[8] period men and older children experienced/experience the world through their imaginations (there is a firm emotional self-sense here, and a growing mental self-sense). And Mental[9] period men and adults – ourselves – experienced/experience the world through their/our ideas (there is a firm mental self-sense here). In the Centauric[10] (postmodern) stage, the self comes to realize that all its individualistic strivings are to little end, and what knowledge it had now slips away as it is realized that reality is beyond the grasp of the discursive intellect.

Wilber's thinking in this area is highly detailed and comparativistic, and in recent years he has made use of the 'Spiral Dynamics' developmental model of Clare Graves, Christopher Cowan, and Don Beck. This model features psychic centres of gravity – forget personality types, here is a consciousness-stage typology with groups given the names of colours. *Beige* refers to the Archaic structure; *Purple*, Magic; *Red*, late Magic-early Mythic; and *Blue*, late Mythic-early Mental. 'Blues' would be Assagioli's ordinary adults – not yet fully rational thinkers, and still tending to ethnocentricity and follow-the-leader conformity. With *Orange* and *Green* referring to the Mental and Centauric stages respectively, 'Oranges' are Mental period men proper, and 'Greens' are postmodernists. Blue is the stage where most people today are 'at', says Wilber. Most *power* today, though, is in the hands of Oranges.

Blues look down on Reds and up to Oranges, says Wilber, although they are uncomfortable with the latter's individualism. Oranges see Green egalitarianism as 'weak and woo-woo',[11] and Greens – if they were to accept such a typology – would see themselves as at the final stage, even though there are higher stages/colours even before we reach the Inward Arc stages. *Yellows* would be thinkers of the still-essentially-materialistic (if in a weak way) 'Systems View' type, says Wilber, and then there are *Turquoises* who are just a sliver away from a genuinely transpersonal/spiritual awareness. Yellows and Turquoises represent the leading edge of collective human evolution today, believes Wilber. We are to understand that each consciousness-stage has a reality content that, in relation to that stage, is 'true'. In effect then, people can't help but see what the stage they're currently at makes them see. (This principle would also apply to people who are at one or other of the transpersonal stages.)

In other works such as *Integral Psychology* (2000), Wilber discusses not just *stages*, but self-related developmental *lines*. One is the *moral* line (connected with identifying first with 'me'; then a friends and family group; then a larger community, racial, religious or national group; then all of humanity; then onto larger wholes). Another relates to *needs* (as in Maslow's hierarchy). The very life of the self is identified with one level of reality after another. Tracing the Outward Arc stages, we have: 1) physical, as I-the-actor (Archaic-Magic); 2) emotional, as I-the-feeler (Magic-Mythic); and 3) mental, as

I-the-thinker (Mythic-Mental). The self's journey involves an identi-fication with one level, then a dis-identification with that level as a new level is identified with. Here is transcendence, says Wilber, but also inclusion/integration.

There can be problems with the new 'take up' part (e.g. a child not fully letting go of the physical self-sense, producing a problem with socialization); and the integration part (e.g. the classic repression of unwanted feelings in the adult – which is a non-integration of the emotional self). 'Intermediate pathologies' include the not letting go of unhealthy group attitudes (script pathologies), and 'higher pathologies' include the non-integration of the lower self by the yogi (spiritual bypassing). A full spectrum therapist is an 'archaeologist of the self', says Wilber (as the personal-spiritual Psychosynthesis therapist is). Recognizing the onward march, should any aspect that has already emerged need attending to, he will duly do so, but as the archaeology is also one that unearths the future, he will also be a spiritual guide. He writes:

> A full-spectrum therapist works with the body, the shadow, the persona, the ego, the existential [Centauric] self, the soul and spirit, attempting to bring awareness to all of them, so that all of them may join consciousness in the extraordinary return voyage of the Self and Spirit that grounds and moves the entire display.[12]

THE INWARD ARC
The Centauric (Transitional)

The Centauric stage is one in which the individual wanders without settling into this worldview (world*form* in mind) or that. The Centauric stage is therefore a trans*membership* state, says Wilber (the postmodernist is not a member of any particular predicative language 'club'), but not a trans*personal* one, for although the Centaur may be highly intuitive and have an 'unqualified sense of relationship', he is still fundamentally grounded in the body (I-as-actor) sense.[13] The Centauric stage does not transcend 'existence, personal orientation, or waking psychophysiological awareness. It is the last stage dominated by normal forms of space and time – but those forms are still there'.[14] In other words, is still Character consciousness, although what we might concede to be a very sensitive and self-possessed (relatively self-actualized) Character consciousness. The Centaur has to go beyond 'meaning in my life' and to let go of self-autonomy, says Wilber. Indeed, the whole point of the Centaur is to 'create a self strong enough to die'. To die to the ordinary self-centred self, that is – to 'let go personal life on the whole'.[15] The Centauric state, or condition, cannot be 'overcome' without spiritual intervention (practising gnosis).

The Low Subtle

'The low-subtle is "composed" of the astral and psychic planes of consciousness', says Wilber.[16] At the Low Subtle stage of transpersonal development, the individual's focus of attention is on this plane as the *most* real dimension of experience. Here we find the first initiate then who, having seen through the illusion of the physical plane, lives in his astral body as his 'centre'.[17] Wilber says that whilst all of us are occasionally transpersonal, here the individual is *ordinarily* 'transpersonally sensitive'. The Low Subtle self is, after the Centaur, a *relatively* enlightened self, says Wilber and – relatedly – the Low Subtle stage is 'probably the most difficult form of the Atman project to break'.[18] We are reminded here of the teaching that the period to be found between the first and second initiations is (or can be) the longest to be found between any two initiations. The *entire realm* of the character's emotions and beliefs has, after all, to be transcended.

The High Subtle

In the High Subtle stage, the individual is confronted with God as the archetypal summit of his own consciousness, says Wilber.[19] In other words, his focus is now on the plane made up of intellects or Cartesian selves (thinking beings), after having seen through the illusion of the emotional plane. This focus translates as the second initiate living in his lower mental body. 'It is the emptiness of everything which allows the identification [here] to take place', says John Blofeld.[20] We are reminded here of Eckhart's meditation on the Nothing, and the work of discrimination that enabled this state of transpersonal development to be attained. 'Consciousness, in a rapid ascent, is [now] differentiating itself entirely from the ordinary mind and self', says Wilber.[21] Here we have the Soul, the second initiate and the Dualistic Mystical State. It is an 'intensification of consciousness', and a blending 'into the object of our contemplation', says Wilber,[22] as the individual at the Sustained Concentration stage of meditation is becoming the soul in the seed-thought.

The Low Causal

> In the high-subtle, recall, the self was dissolved or reabsorbed into the archetypal deity, as that deity – a deity which from the beginning has always been one's own Self and highest archetype. Now at the low causal, that deity-Archetype itself condenses and dissolves into final-God, which is here seen as an extraordinarily subtle audible-light.
>
> Ken Wilber[23]

If each of Wilber's five stages of transpersonal development are linked to the five occult initiations, then we may expect that the Low Causal structure is the 'mindset' of the third initiate. We said earlier that the third initiate lives in his Causal Body (Seat of Solomon, Temple of Christ, etc.), having seen through the illusion of the lower mental plane – the plane made up of original and individual creatures of mind. To transcend this *is* to be dissolved back into 'final-God' as the *Universal* Mind-self. This is the first aspect of the soul initially glimpsed in the PCE; now, just as the Monad is fully experienced at the fifth initiation, the soul is fully experienced here as a 'light-body' (it should be understood that Wilber is essentially looking at the phenomenal content of a mystic's awareness). This light-body is not yours or mine: it is the light of the soul 'overlighting' the light of the personality. The Low Causal stage is therefore where personality-consciousness and soul-consciousness are integrated.

The adult is conscious of being a definite individual being with specific characteristics and an objective body. I have an I-sense (I can say with Descartes: I can doubt everything, but not the existence of me-who-doubts); I have a personality-sense (I know I like some foods and people, but not others); and I have a body-sense. This last is the strongest because it is the *oldest*, and my ego is most heavily invested in this accordingly. But what if I became aware that the physical world was not an objective realm – that cold hard matter was a lie, making my individual existence as a discrete body, confirmed by science and affirmed by my child consciousness, an illusion? I would then be forced to look for confirmation of my individual existence from religion/non-materialistic science, and affirmation from my adolescent consciousness. This is the Low Subtle stage of evolution. What if I now became aware that my individual existence as a personality was an illusion? I would then be forced to look for affirmation of my individual existence from my specifically adult consciousness. This is the High Subtle stage of evolution. What if I now became aware that my individual existence as an 'I' – a Cartesian self – was an illusion? My self-sense would then have dissolved back into 'final-God'. Beyond me-as-body, me-as-personality, and me-as-me, lies 'me-as-God'.[24] This is the Low Causal stage.

Wilber's six basic levels of reality (Wilber has his own under-standing of the perennial philosophy, or at least a multilevelled universe) are: 1) matter, 2) living body, 3) mind, 4) soul, 5) spirit, and 6) God. At each stage the self's locus of identification is at a certain level – Mental (matter), Low Subtle (living body), High Subtle (mind), Low Causal (soul), High Causal (spirit), and Ultimate (God). The Theosophical arrangement would be Mental (physical), Low Subtle (emotional), High Subtle (lower mental), Low Causal (higher mental), High Causal (buddhic), and Ultimate (atmic). If Yellow or

Turquoise is the stage where a lot of people are at today, then they're on the cusp of having a locus of identification at the next level up – the living matter or emotional level.

The High Causal

'This is total and utter transcendence and release into Formless Consciousness', says Wilber.[25] This refers to the mindset of the fourth initiate[26] for whom the personal self-as-soul (or personal archetype as Final-God) no longer exists. The soul part still does, but not the ego-centricity. 'Both subject and object are [here] forgotten', says Wilber,[27] which translates as the individual no longer seeing himself *as a person*, in any form – 'high' or 'low'. The fourth initiate, recall, sits in the airport and writes his letters of farewell, whilst looking up at the departures board. 'There is only radiance [here]', says Wilber,[28] which translates as the individual living in his buddhic vehicle, as the Son who knows he is one with the Father, and only waits for this to be *completely* so in his experience. This is the stage of 'transcendent love-in-oneness', says Wilber.[29] This is the fourth initiate Besant recognizes who 'stands robed in that glorious vesture of unchanging peace that naught can mar'.[30] The Work of the Night has been followed by the Work of the Dawn, and a nice sunny Day is promised.

The Ultimate Stage

> [Here] Consciousness totally awakes as its Original Condition and Suchness (*tathata*), which is, at the same time, the condition and suchness of all that is, gross, subtle, or causal. That which witnesses, and that which is witnessed, are only one and the same. The entire World Process then arises, moment to moment, as one's own Being, outside of which, and prior to which, nothing exists. That Being is totally beyond and prior to anything that arises, and yet no part of that Being is other than what arises.

Ken Wilber[31]

It might be incorrect to call this a stage, because this is beyond the finish line of transpersonal (but not, as we have seen, initiatory) development. Here, that which witnesses, and that which is witnessed, are only one and the same (the Whole looking out from behind the individual's eyes at Itself). 'Consciousness', in this quote, refers to the Son, and its 'original condition and suchness' is the Father as the body-consciousness of our Planetary Man, theosophically understood. The fifth initiate has 'moved on' to planetary concerns; thus his level of concern is that of the 'entire world process'. This life of our planetary being eclipses the lives of human and subhuman beings, whether we have in mind their gross (personality), subtle (soul), or causal (spirit) natures. This Being is totally beyond and prior to anything that arises in the realms of strictly human and subhuman experience – as the author is with respect to the characters in his play.

13 Challenges of the Esoteric View

THE CHALLENGE OF THE NEW SAME UNIVERSE

We have used both the analogy of man as a character in a play, and the image of gnosis as the lifting of a veil to reveal an alternate reality – one which is always there and staring us in the face, but which we are blind to. This alternate reality would be the occult, as in supernatural, as in of-another-kind-of-natural reality. *Another kind of natural would still be natural.* The spiritual path is about becoming a new oneself, as opposed to a new, as in different, as in other self. The esotericist sees what we might call a 'new same' universe. He would say it is a more 'obvious' universe, featuring planetary and solar entities which are 'of course' bigger in life and consciousness than the human, and galactic and supergalactic entities which are of course bigger in life and consciousness than the planetary and solar. We might try to imagine the qualitative difference between the *experience* of a wood tick and ourselves, and then continue in the same expanding direction, says Huston Smith. The initiatory journey leads far away from the beaten track of humans, but brings us back to exactly where we began – to that *present all along*, says Peter Kingsley.

> Metaphysically, human reality is reducible to the Divine
> Reality and in itself is only illusory; theologically, Divine

> Reality is in appearance reduced to human reality, in the
> sense that It does not surpass the latter in existential but
> only in causal quality.
>
> Frithjof Schuon[1]

An *esoteric* universe? Yes, but only from one angle. And where we might speak of Superbia as the domain of a new, higher-than-human kingdom in terms of awareness, this is so, again, only from one angle. The esoteric teaching, in the final analysis, is that the spiritual (and being spiritual), is really just the 'highest' *normal* (and being the highest normal). Esotericism is dualistic (esoteric reality/exoteric reality), but then again it would not be incorrect to say that esotericism is monistic. An esotericist would accept the charge of being a monotheist, referring to the Absolute behind any and all logoic systems, and/or the highest Cosmic Logos, and/or our 'local' God as the body-consciousness of our Planetary or Solar Man. Also a tritheist, with the Logos being a three-in-one Logos. And a polytheist, with there being many Logoi. And even a kathenotheist, in the sense that when we reach the top of *our* mountain, it stands revealed to us as just a grain of sand forming part of a sandy plain with yet another mountain before us – a pictorial way of referring to solar and cosmic planes.

Then again, an esotericist would accept the charge of being a pantheist, with the universe being divine. And a panentheist, with there being an Absolute behind this divine universe. Even an atheist, with respect to the of-another-kind-of-natural universe. In the end, there is no philosophical position of esotericism. We might want it to wear conceptual shoes and walk our world-of-thought roads, but it remains barefoot and travels along natural lines. All of this is to the complete frustration of the ordinary cataloguer of views of course, and the breaking-up-into-dissimilars analytical mind. Small wonder then, that it has taken so long for Western Esotericism to be born as an academic discipline – perhaps awaiting the sophisticated, 'hyper-intellectual' aptitude to get a handle on it. 'It' here not being what is esoteric, but what is, on the face of it, the 'madness' of esotericism's omnidirectional metaphysical assertions and discourses. The making sense of these was the principle aim of this work, giving (to the best of the author's ability) a comprehensive and comprehensible picture of the esoteric worldview.

THE CHALLENGE OF THE PERENNIAL PHILOSOPHY

A description of China is not China. A map of China distilled from a thousand descriptions of China, is still not China. To know China one has to go there, and to know the perennial philosophy *as* Divine Reality, one has to 'go there' too. In the writings of many contemporary thinkers, the perennial philosophy is essentially the premodern worldview – a philosophical consensus of sorts, featuring a multi-levelled universe from matter, through living systems, mind and soul, to spirit/God. This gives us a perennial philosophy 'map' of sorts but, reminds esotericism, we are to remember that the map is not the terrain. Moreover, the map may only refer to *part* of the terrain anyway, depending on how far into the territory the majority of travellers went, and/or what they were able or thought necessary to express – considering the rest of us and our ordinary religious languages and experiential frames of reference.

When enlightenment is spoken of in mystical traditions, it is the sharing in the body-consciousness of our Planetary Man that is commonly being referred to, says Theosophy. This is a *relative* enlightenment, and this God is our *initial* ontological-cosmogenetic 'context'. God in the 'standard' map therefore refers to *a* God, but not the *highest* God. And we have not just *our* levels of being to consider: the standard perennial philosophy map is really or at best only a perennial *psychology*, as in psyche-ology, as in *our-cosmos-system-only*, map. Perhaps there was no reason in the *past* for a map with more than just our mountain on it. But equally *now* – as we are (if we are) beginning to collectively wake up from our Character illusion (and enter the Space Age) – there is.

To know the perennial philosophy as Divine Reality requires

engaging in the gnostic project, and there is perhaps evidence today that many philosophers are 'fulfilling the necessary conditions'. Iamblichus cautioned against a purely intellectual approach i.e. one not accompanied by moral purification and mystical practice (this is the message to esoterologists). We mustn't forget the *constant* periphery-centre relationship, said Frithjof Schuon (this is the message to the evolutionist thinker). Jacob Boehme said that none should think or desire to find the lily of the heavenly bud with deep searching and studying, if he not be entered by earnest repentance in the New Birth, so that it be grown in himself (this is the message to all of us).

The only means of knowing what is, as opposed to knowing ideas on what is, is gnosis. There seems to be broad consensus today that we need a new map – a new *Naturphilosophie* that, as Antoine Faivre says, would 'associate the flesh with the flame'.[2] Upon the dissemination and general acceptance of this, the ideal society (or at least a better one) depends. But esotericism cautions: We mustn't just take the old map and, 'casually' qualifying it as the premodern worldview, modernize it to accommodate modern scientific (quantitative) findings and methodology. Heindel wrote of the 'Religion of the Father' to come after the (present) 'Religion of the Son'.[3] This refers to an understanding of spirit and *its* context (the new same universe), after an understanding of the soul (consciousness) and its context (the usual Atman-Brahman).

THE CHALLENGE OF THE SUN

The challenge of the sun is also the challenge of the earth, other cosmic 'objects', and the interpretation of the archaic Mysteries. In Theosophical writings we see three suns commonly referred to: 1) the ordinary physical sun we see; 2) our Solar Logos as God; and 3) a Solar Man on cosmic planes. Another sun (4) would be the Sun in the archaic Mysteries, which is the *symbolic* name for a principle/body/centre (the soul centre – Tiphereth in Kabbalism). Yet another sun (5) would be the sun as a symbol – an archetype – of the higher self (either as the soul, or – as in Alchemy – the spirit). Only suns (1) and (5) would appear to be recognized by thinkers of the Transpersonal type, and therefore there is *a* new universe-picture, which is really but a layering over of the ordinary materialist picture (with suns and planets, not to mention other cosmic entities, not awarded an ontological status 'higher' than man's). Cosmic *objects* of different sizes, yes; cosmic *psyches* of different sizes, with man's highest consciousness potential but a sharing in the body-consciousness of a planetary or solar being already present, no. There would appear to be five primary concerns of esotericism with respect to this picture:

1 There is no Atman/Brahman as the Monad/
body-consciousness of our Planetary Man.
2 There are no consciousness-beings/planes all the way up.
3 There are no levels of logoic systems, with a simultaneity of dot-line-circle systems.
4 There is a tendency to simply put the Great Chain of Being on its side, recognizing consciousness evolution but not spiritual Aevertinity. (Some followers of Traditionalism, it has to be said, have the opposite tendency).
5 Without a 'vertical', *here-and-now* Divine Reality appreciated, it is difficult for a Superbia (a 'Kingdom of God') – and maybe also a returning 'World Teacher' from it (the hope and teaching of many world religions) – to be accepted.

To be clear, the concern is with what might be called the standard new paradigm picture, in which there are the *ideas* of holarchy, *autopoiesis* (self-creation), self-organization, and qualitative evolution – as there are in the esoteric picture. Esotericism's holarchy, though, refers to a hierarchy of sentient god-beings; autopoiesis and self-organization refer to logoic-systems (dot-line-circle systems which self-originate, and then 'work themselves out'); and qualitative evolution is intellectually inscrutable and has as its backdrop the Aevertinal. 'Thou must elevate the mind in the *spirit*, and consider how the *whole nature* ... is together the *body* [body-consciousness] ... of God', wrote Jacob

Boehme[4] (see next section on the five-dimensional). An aspect uncommonly discussed is that a perennial philosophy must be time-proof i.e. not only have been true a thousand or a billion years ago, but be true in a thousand or a billion years time. Any scheme which puts itself forward as *the* Grand Design, and which is attached to a quantitative or Character-science, *by* this attachment, can't be the big picture (even if it is an 'improved' picture).

THE CHALLENGE OF TIME AND MAYA

The very existence of the Characters' minds is down to, and is contained within, the consciousness of their author, says esotericism. Here is the challenge of time and Maya. 'The rationalistic view forgets entirely that everything which it may express concerning the universe, *remains a content of human consciousness*', says Titus Burckhardt.[5] And Schuon says: 'Profane science, in seeking to pierce to its depths the mystery of the things that contain – space, time, matter, energy – forgets the mystery of the things *that are contained*.'[6] Reality has us in its grasp and always has. We may read the 'new physics' (which posits or entertains *some kind* of divine ground behind the sensible universe) in the light of revealed Tradition, says Antoine Faivre, but we 'pass unjustly from a metaphysics born of a new epistemology [true philosophy] to a "gnosis" born of the result of experiments carried out by the mere "eyes of the flesh"'.[7] These being the Character's eyes.

Man is an automaton – from the point of view of the enlightened self, the 'previous' self wasn't really alive. There would be a new same *life* that goes with the new same universe, and this universe is located in Aevertinity. 'The body [the Character] can know only the body [its world]; the soul can know only the soul; the spirit can know only the spirit', said Rudolf Steiner.[8] There is the idea of three-dimensional awareness (the ordinary 'fictional' world seen); four-dimensional awareness (the soul seen – this refers to Consciousness-time, and the 'space' that goes with that, which is the environment of Soul(s)); and five-dimensional awareness (spirit seen – this refers to Aevertinity and the space that goes with that, which is the new same universe). The challenge of time is, really, the challenge of dimensional awareness. And the challenge of Maya is the challenge of the new same universe and a correct life-to-life relationship with it. Says Purucker on this:

> When man feels himself at-one with all that is: when he feels that the consciousness which he calls his own is but a god-spark, so to say, of some vaster Consciousness, in which he lives; and that the very atoms which compose his own body are built of infinitesimal lives which in-fill those atoms and make them what they are; when he feels that he can pass along the pathways of his own spirit ever more and more inwards into a closer and straighter union with some self-conscious Entity still more sublime than his own highest: then he feels not only a keen sense of his own high human dignity, but he looks out upon the universe around him, and his heart then broadens, and his mind expands, in sympathy, love, and benevolence towards all other beings and entities and things. Vast sweeps of consciousness open up for him as being his own future; duty takes on a new and gloriously bright aspect; right becomes the law of his living, and ethics no longer are a more or less tiresome code of abstract teaching, but very living and vital maxims of conduct.[9]

The goal is to 'bring the kingdoms of the earth into harmonic concord with the kingdom of space', wrote Manly Hall.[10] The challenges of the esoteric view presented here are, we can see, fundamental and interrelated. Much of esotericism is psychological – that is to say, has to do with our cosmos-system; but esotericism goes further than that which simply lies at the end of *our* Hermetic line. There are Gods – consciousness-beings and logoic-systems – all the way up, and esotericism's map features spirit in *its* context, not just consciousness in its context. Esotericism also acknowledges that at some point mysticism turns into occultism, and the gnoseology postgraduate becomes (this making him a gnoseology doctor) a true cosmologist.

To repeat the point earlier made, the problem with some followers of Traditionalism is a tendency to see only the snapshot Aevertinal picture featuring God and immediate spiritual energies, and not the psychic reality of consciousness evolution. There has therefore, in their view, simply been a degeneration of human civilization – not also a 'progress' in psychic terms. The problem with the purely evolutionist thinker is a tendency to see only material or psychic evolution (if the latter, layered over a quantitative cosmology and material cosmogenesis), and not the Aevertinal or vertical here-and-now universe. It is *not* a case of a static Great Chain *or* evolution, says esotericism, but *both*. And the problem with some scholars of Western Esotericism – who might otherwise simply affirm these *conceptual* challenges – is precisely what Iamblichus cautioned against. The author entertains a future in which there is a 'blue sky esotericism', devoid of doctrinairism and concordism, mystification, and empty analysis – being grounded in the awareness of the new same universe that is.

> Give ear to me who pray that I may never of Gnosis fail,
> which is our common being's nature; and fill me with Thy
> Power, and with this Grace of Thine, that I may give the
> Light to those in ignorance of the Race, my Brethren, and
> Thy Sons. For this cause I believe, and I bear witness; I go
> to Life and Light. Blessed art Thou, O Father. Thy Man
> would holy be as Thou art holy, even as Thou gave him Thy
> full authority to be.
>
> From *Poemandres*[11]

Notes

INTRODUCTION

1   Some scholars prefer the term 'Hermetism' – at least to refer to Alexandrian Hermes-ism.

2   The reader is referred here instead to the standard reference works: Antoine Faivre and Jacob Needleman, eds., *Modern Esoteric Spirituality* (New York: The Crossroad Publishing Company, 1992); and Wouter J Hanegraaff, ed., in collaboration with Antoine Faivre, Roelof van den Broek and Jean-Pierre Brach, *Dictionary of Gnosis and Western Esotericism* (Leiden: E J Brill, 2005).

3   W T S Thackara, 'The Perennial Philosophy', *Sunrise: Theosophical Perspectives*, April/May 1984, http://www.theosociety.org/pasadena/sunrise/33-83-4/ge-wtst.htm.

4   Frances A Yates, *Giordano Bruno and the Hermetic Tradition* (New York: Random House, 1969), 14.

5   Aldous Huxley, *The Perennial Philosophy* (New York: Harper & Row, 1990), viii-ix.

6   Ibid., 34.

7   Ibid., 33.

8   Ibid., 21.

9   Wouter J Hanegraaff, 'Some Remarks on the Study of Western Esotericism', *Esoterica*, Volume 1, 1999, http://www.esoteric.msu.edu/hanegraaff.html.

10 Antoine Faivre, *Access to Western Esotericism* (Albany, NY: State University of New York Press, 1994), 10. In the thought of Pierre Riffard, an esoterologist would be the scholar who follows the 'external method' to a knowledge of esotericism, whereas the 'esoterosophist' would be the individual who follows the 'internal method' (See 'The Esoteric Method' in Antoine Faivre and Wouter J Hanegraaff, eds., *Western Esotericism and the Science of Religion*, Leuven: Peeters, 1998, 63-74).

11 Arthur Versluis, 'Mysticism, and the Study of Esotericism: Methods in the Study of Esotericism, Part II', *Esoterica*, Volume 5, 2003, http://www.esoteric.msu.edu/volumev/mysticism.htm.

12 Quoted in Basarab Nicolescu, *Science, Meaning, & Evolution: The Cosmology of Jacob Boehme* (New York: Parabola Books, 1991), 15.

13 Jacob Needleman, 'Introduction II', in Antoine Faivre and Jacob Needleman, eds., *Modern Esoteric Spirituality* (London: SCM Press Ltd, 1993), xxv.

14 Hanegraaff, 'Some Remarks on the Study of Western Esotericism'.

15 William W Quinn, Jr., *The Only Tradition* (Albany, NY: State University of New York Press, 1997), 343.

16 Ibid., 339.

17 Versluis, 'Mysticism, and the Study of Esotericism: Methods in the Study of Esotericism, Part II'.

18 Antoine Faivre led the way in offering a definition of esotericism as a field of enquiry (see *Access to Western Esotericism*, 3-35). All such definitions of what themes or concerns together constitute esotericism as a 'form of thought' (to use Faivre's phrase) can be debated and used heuristically of course i.e. they are useful intradisciplinarily. But this is still orbiting the real material. Kocku von Stuckrad has proposed that instead of an esotericism of the systemic type, we think of an 'esoteric field of discourse' in Western cultural self-expression. This would serve the purpose of not – from the outset – setting apart esotericism from traditional religion, science, and philosophy, thereby enabling us to appreciate 'the complexity of European cultural history, without playing off religion against science, Christianity against paganism, or reason against superstition' (Kocku von Stuckrad, *Western Esotericism: A Brief History of Secret Knowledge*, London: Equinox, 2005, 6-11). We can identify the strong influence of continental philosophy here, which centripetally moves towards the irreducibility of human subjectivity (see also note 20 below) and especially the politics of language. There is nothing wrong with this 'continental' approach per se, but when it comes to a suitable starting point for the study of esotericism, the postmodernization of the discipline mustn't be allowed to close or deny the door through which the *practitioner*-scholar egresses and returns with 'knowledge by identity' as opposed to merely 'knowledge about' (for a discussion of this see Robert K C Forman, *Mysticism, Mind, Consciousness*, Albany, NY: State University of New York Press, 1999, 10-127).

19 Jean d'Espagnet, *The Hermetic Arcanum* [1623], The Alchemy Web Site, http://www.alchemywebsite.com/harcanum.html.

20 In his book *Philosophy in World Perspective: A Comparative Hermeneutic of the Major Theories* (New Haven and London: Yale University Press, 1989), Dilworth identifies four perspectival voices in philosophy. The first is the *objective*: This is the voice of realism, which affirms the existence of an observer-independent reality. The second is the *personal*: This is the voice of existentialism, which affirms the irreducibility of human subjectivity. The third is the *disciplinary*: This is the voice of analysism, which affirms the non-finality of the philosophical project. And the fourth is the *diaphanic*: This is the voice of religionism, which affirms the existence of a God and an ultimate truth. Features of diaphanic expression include: a) the making of authoritative assertions without (necessarily) providing empirical, testimonial, or argumentative support; and b) appealing to the reader's 'higher nature' for an understanding (and therewith also acceptance) of the author's intention and meaning. Western philosophers who have employed diaphanic expression include Plato, Plotinus, Hegel, Spinoza, and Schelling, says Dilworth, but the tradition of diaphanic expression goes back further than written philosophy because it is 'the standard voice of religious texts' (ibid., 27). Most philosophy and religious studies departments today resound with the disciplinary voice. This is because in the perceived absence of a final 'destination' (God) and ultimate truth (perennial philosophy), the searchlight of the human mind must be directed at its own creations. Students are thus taught to always critically analyse and contextualize views. But as Huston Smith says in *Beyond the Postmodern Mind* (Wheaton, IL: Quest Books, 1996), the fundamental job of a civilization's centres of learning is to keep that civilization *vital*. This can only be done if the 'high image of man' [that is, as essentially divine] is kept alive (ibid., 120). This is precisely what is *not* happening today because and when our universities insist on critical thinking and disciplinary expression, to the exclusion of spiritual insight and diaphanic expression.

21 The author would agree with Hanegraaff that a 'first necessary step towards establishing the study of esotericism as a serious academic pursuit would be to demarcate it clearly from the perennialist perspective' ('On the Construction of "Esoteric Traditions"' in *Western Esotericism and the Science of Religion*, 27). This is where that perennialist perspective is the one that rejects esotericism *outside* of the major (revealed) religions, and therefore sees the teachings of 'occult schools' as pseudo-esotericism (or –esoter*ism*). The author is strongly sympathetic to the perennialist/Traditionalist view, as will be evident from the tenor of this book; however, there is a strong doctrinairist tendency in Traditionalism – a tendency to substitute philosophical principles *for that which they merely point towards and*

which are discovered through gnostic practice. 'A finger is required to point at the moon, but when the moon is recognized, the finger is no longer required', says a Zen proverb. The 'finger' that is the principle of the 'transcendent unity of religions' merely points towards the esoteric being found in the religious – which is an *orientation* manifested in literature and elsewhere. It is *not* the case that the esoteric is to be found only in the major religions – it is on this erroneous basis that Whitall N Perry, for instance, dismisses H P Blavatsky and G I Gurdjieff ('The Revival of Interest in Tradition' in Ranjit Fernando, ed., *The Unanimous Tradition: Essays on the Essential Unity of All Religions*, Colombo: The Sri Lanka Institute of Traditional Studies, 1991, 16). Back to Hanegraaff, the perennialist perspective that is *not* doctrinairist though – which simply affirms the reality of the Divine Intellect (and by extension a Divine corpus of knowledge, to seek which is the pursuit par excellence) – is a view entirely in keeping with the origins and thrust of the Western philosophical tradition.

CHAPTER 1 – EARLY ESOTERICISM

1   'The implication of the Nicene doctrine', writes Joseph Macchio, 'is that Jesus as God the Logos, God Himself, simply assumed a human nature and body (or the semblance of humanity) for the purpose of saving mankind. He himself did not need to follow a path to attainment, nor did he have to strive for union with God. Jesus then was not really man – he was the eternal God in the appearance of man.' He continues: 'The above formula also makes it unnecessary for each individual to follow Jesus. There is no purpose in seeking to experience the 'initiations' that Jesus experienced. The esoteric Gnostic doctrines of Jesus, *which taught man how to attain to Jesus's level of spiritual knowledge and power*, are now become superfluous.' (Joseph P. Macchio, *The Orthodox Suppression of Original Christianity*, 2003, www.essenes.net/conspireindex.html). Superfluous, and henceforth heretical teachings. The result over subsequent centuries was the destruction of many Gnostic (and Hermetic) writings, and the persecution of many Gnostic/Hermetic groups, whose teachings and very existence threatened the authority and power of the Church. The Council of Nicea took place during the reign of the Christian Roman Emperor Constantine (272-337). His successor Julian (331-363) was the last pagan Emperor of Rome, and a champion particularly of Neoplatonism and Chaldeanism as we see in his *Oration upon the Sovereign Sun* (c351) and other works. Another important date in our history is 869, when the 8th Ecumenical Council ruled that man was a duality of body and soul, not a triplicity of body, soul, and spirit (only Christ was that).

Together with St Augustine's doctrine of original sin then, we had: a) Jesus Christ was essentially divine (we are not); b) we are, in fact, intrinsically sinners; and c) our only salvation lies through faith (not gnosis), and following the edicts of the Church (not our own Christ-like natures).

2   Stephan A Hoeller, *Gnosticism: New Light on the Ancient Tradition of Inner Knowing* (Wheaton, IL: Quest Books, 2002), 188.

3   David Brons, 'The Valentinian View of the Creation', 2003, http://www.gnosis.org/library/valentinus/Valentinian_Creation.htm.

4   Manly P Hall, *Journey in Truth* (Los Angeles: Philosophical Research Society, 1945), 49.

5   Manly P Hall, *Lectures on Ancient Philosophy: An Introduction to Practical Ideals* (Los Angeles: Philosophical Research Society, 1984), 272.

6   Peter Kingsley, *Reality* (Inverness, CA: The Golden Sufi Center Publishing, 2003), 359-60.

7   Manly P Hall, *The Wisdom of the Knowing Ones: Gnosticism: The Key to Esoteric Christianity* (Los Angeles: Philosophical Research Society, 2000), 116.

8   Antoine Faivre, 'Ancient and Medieval Sources of Modern Esoteric Movements', in *Modern Esoteric Spirituality*, 11.

9   The *Corpus Hermeticum* forms part of the wider body of Hermetic writings, the *Hermetica*, which includes the *Tabula Smaragdina Hermetis* (Emerald Tablet of Hermes).

10 Gilles Quispel, 'The Asclepius: From the Hermetic Lodge in Alexandria to the Greek Eucharist and the Roman Mass.' In Roelof van den Broek and Wouter J Hanegraaff, eds., *Gnosis and Hermeticism from Antiquity to Modern Times* (Albany, NY: State University of New York Press, 1998), 74.

11 G R S Mead, [1906] *Thrice Greatest Hermes: Studies in Hellenistic Theosophy and Gnosis*, The Gnostic Society Library, http://www.gnosis.org/library/hermes10.html.

12 Quoted in David Loy, *Nonduality: A Study in Comparative Philosophy* (Atlantic Highlands, NJ: Humanities Press International, 1997), 1.

CHAPTER 2 – TRADITIONALISM

1   The name Rosicrucianism derives from a Christian Rosenkreuz ('Rose Cross') – a Hermetic teacher who may have lived in the 14th century, but whose name is symbolic anyway, and whose story and teachings appeared in a series of texts that emerged in the early 17th century. Rosicrucianists believe in a tradition of ancient and

trans-Western origin, which is guarded by an assembly of Adepts.

2   Martinism derives historically from the theurgic school and system, called *Elus Cohen*, of Martines de Pasqually (1727-1774), and from the mystic philosophy of his pupil Louis-Claude de Saint-Martin (1743-1803). Both were, purportedly, heirs to an initiatic Hermetic-Christian tradition that extended through the Cathars and the Knights Templars. Later, Gérard Encausse, alias Papus (1865-1915), established a Martinist Order that taught of an Inner Way of reintegration (of consciousness).

3   In 1993 there was a further Parliament of the World's Religions which produced a declaration 'Towards a Global Ethic', and in 1999 another, which produced the declaration 'A Call to Our Guiding Institutions'. Conference participants were asked to delve deep into their own religious traditions to bring wisdom (not doctrine) to the table, and to focus on the question of what was to be done in the face of the world's evils and suffering (not on what the relations were between the different religions). The intention was to unify at the level of ethics and pragmatic action. The spirit of the Interfaith Movement generally is one that rejects syncretism as well as relativism and indifferentism, and some 'interfaithers' believe that unity is achievable through our common trans-faith spirituality, whilst others believe it will come about through a common struggle against war, poverty, environmental spoliation, and injustice. Unlike 'official' interreligious discussions, where the host organization may have its own agenda, interfaith organizations do not (in a manner of speaking) send out invitations all from the same address.

4   Richard Tarnas, *The Passion of the Western Mind: Understanding the Ideas That Have Shaped Our World View* (London: Pimlico, 1996), 310.

5   Jean Borella, 'René Guénon and the Traditionalist School', in *Modern Esoteric Spirituality*, 331.

6   William W Quinn, Jr., *The Only Tradition*, 44.

7   Mead, *Thrice Greatest Hermes*, http://www.gnosis.org/library/hermes5.html.

8   Frithjof Schuon, 'Sophia Perennis and the Theory of Evolution and Progress', 2001, http://www.frithjof-schuon.com/evolution-engl.htm.

9   Philip Sherrard, 'How Do I See the Universe and Man's Place in It?' (paper presented at the conference on Modern Science and Traditional Religions Consultation, Windsor, England, March 1976), http://www.incommunion.org/articles/older-issues/the-universe-and-mans-place-in-it.

10 Smith, *Beyond the Postmodern Mind*, 157.

11 Schuon, 'Sophia Perennis'.

12 Ananda K Coomaraswamy, *Selected Papers: Metaphysics* (Princeton, NJ: Princeton University Press, 1977), 14.

13 Smith, *Beyond the Postmodern Mind*, 53-4.

14 Frithjof Schuon, *Light on the Ancient Worlds* (Bloomington, IN: World Wisdom Books, 1984), 111.

15 Smith, *Beyond the Postmodern Mind*, 66.

16 James S Cutsinger, 'An Open Letter on Tradition', 2001, http://www.cutsinger.net/pdf/letter.pdf.

17 To be clear, 'gnoseology' as used here (and in the rest of the book) means the science of gnosis, not epistemology.

18 Quoted in Fernando, *The Unanimous Tradition*, 19.

19 Julius Evola, 'On the Secret of Degeneration', *Deutsches Volkstum*, Number 11, 1938, http://pages.zoom.co.uk/thuban/html/evola.html.

20 Allan Combs, *The Radiance of Being: Complexity, Chaos and the Evolution of Consciousness* (St. Paul, MN: Paragon House, 1996), 75.

21 René Guénon, *The Reign of Quantity and The Signs of the Times* (London: Luzac & Company, 1953), 233.

22 Ibid., 352, emphasis mine.

23 Frithjof Schuon, *The Transcendent Unity of Religions* (Wheaton, IL: Quest Books, 1993), 3.

24 Ibid., 14.

25 Schuon, 'Sophia Perennis'.

CHAPTER 3 – THEOSOPHY

1 Quinn, *The Only Tradition*, 113.

2 Alice A Bailey, *Initiation, Human and Solar* (London and New York: Lucis Trust, 1992), x.

3 Joscelyn Godwin, *The Theosophical Enlightenment* (Albany, NY: State University of New York Press, 1994), 377.

4 Antoine Faivre, *Theosophy, Imagination, Tradition: Studies in Western Esotericism* (Albany, NY: State University of New York Press, 2000), 20.

5 Godwin, *The Theosophical Enlightenment*, 379.

6 For a brief account of the origins and divisions of the Theosophical Society, see Robert Ellwood, *Theosophy: A Modern Expression of the Wisdom of the Ages* (Wheaton, IL: Quest Books), 211-16.

7 G de Purucker, *The Esoteric Tradition* (Pasadena, CA: Theosophical University Press, 1940), chap. 6, http://www.theosociety.org/pasadena/et/et-6.htm.

8 Quoted in Franz Hartmann, *The Life of Paracelsus and the Substance*

of his Teachings (San Diego: Wizards Bookshelf, 1985), 196.

9   Heinrich Cornelius Agrippa, *De Occulta Philosophia* (digital edition by Joseph H Peterson, 2000), book II, part 2, chap. LV, http://www.esotericarchives.com/agrippa/agripp2d.htm.

10 Hall, *Lectures on Ancient Philosophy*, 29.

11 H P Blavatsky, [1888] *The Secret Doctrine: The Synthesis of Science, Religion, and Philosophy* (Pasadena, CA: Theosophical University Press, 1988), vol. I. 594.

12 Alice A Bailey, *A Treatise on Cosmic Fire* (London and New York: Lucis Trust, 1989), 272.

13 Ibid., 257.

14 Brett Mitchell, *The Sun is Alive: The Spirit, Consciousness, and Intelligence of our Solar System* (Carlsbad, CA: Esoteric Publishing, 1997), 94.

15 Blavatsky, *The Secret Doctrine*, vol. I, 39.

16 Max Heindel, *The Rosicrucian Cosmo-Conception or Mystic Christianity* (Oceanside, CA: The Rosicrucian Fellowship, 1992), 179.

17 Huston Smith, *The World's Religions: Our Great Wisdom Traditions* (New York: HarperCollins, 2001), 72.

18 Blavatsky, *The Secret Doctrine*, vol. I, 40.

19 Annie Besant, *The Ancient Wisdom: An Outline of Theosophical Teachings* (Adyar, Madras: The Theosophical Publishing House), 37.

20 Blavatsky, *The Secret Doctrine*, Vol. I, 542.

21 Sri Krishna Prem, *The Yoga of the Bhagavat Gita* (London: John Watkins, 1958), 196.

22 Alice A Bailey, *A Treatise on White Magic or The Way of the Disciple* (London and New York: Lucis Trust, 1991), 339.

23 Sherrard, 'How Do I See the Universe.'

24 Blavatsky, *The Secret Doctrine*, Vol. I, 633.

25 Ibid., 520, emphasis mine.

26 Ibid., 107.

27 Hall, *Lectures on Ancient Philosophy*, 416.

28 The Eighth is the *Ogdoad*; the Ninth is the *Ennead*. These are two of the ten Pythagorean numbers. From 1-10: *Monad, Duad, Triad, Tetrad, Pentad, Hexad, Heptad, Ogdoad, Ennead, Decad*. The Empyrean is also the *Primum Mobile* (sphere of the 'Prime Mover') in Ptolemaic astronomy – the tenth if we consider the Earth the first, then the planets (second to eighth), then the stars (ninth).

29 G de Purucker, *The Doctrine of the Spheres*, Vol. VII, *Esoteric Teachings* (San Diego, CA: Point Loma Publications, 1987), 44.

CHAPTER 4 – SOME OTHER ESOTERIC SCHOOLS

1 Jacob Boehme, [1622] *Of Regeneration, or the New Birth*, chap. 6, Christian Classics Ethereal Library, http://www.ccel.org/b/boehme/way/regeneration.html.

2 See Arthur Versluis, *Wisdom's Children: A Christian Esoteric Tradition* (Albany, NY: State University of New York Press, 1999), 323-24.

3 Ibid., 132.

4 Quoted in Ibid.

5 Ibid., 290.

6 Quoted in Nicolescu, *Science, Meaning, & Evolution*, 230.

7 Jacob Boehme, [1622] *The Supersensual Life, or The Life Which is Above Sense*, first dialogue, Christian Classics Ethereal Library, http://www.ccel.org/b/boehme/way/supersensual_life.html.

8 Ibid.

9 Ibid., second dialogue.

10 Versluis, *Wisdom's Children*, 145.

11 Boehme, *Of Regeneration*, chap. 8.

12 Ibid., chap. 4.

13 Nicholas Goodrick-Clarke, ed., *Helena Blavatsky* (Berkeley, CA: North Atlantic Books, 2004), 176.

14 Gershom Scholem, *Major Trends in Jewish Mysticism* (New York: Schocken, 1961), 398-99.

15 Leo Schaya, 'Some Universal Aspects of Judaism', in *The Unanimous Tradition*, 60.

16 Z'ev ben Shimon Halevi, *The Way of the Kabbalah* (Boston, MA: Weiser, 1976), 85.

17 Ibid., 213.

18 Y Ashlag, 'The Teachings of the Ten Sefirot', Bnei Baruch World Center for Kabbalah Studies, 1996, http://www.kabbalah.info/engkab/commentary.htm.

19 Antoine-Joseph Pernety, [1758?] *A Treatise on The Great Art: A System of Physics According to Hermetic Philosophy and Theory and Practice of the Magisterium* (e-book edition by Flaming Sword Productions, 1997, 12), http://www.hermetics.org/pdf/alchemy/The_Great_Art.pdf.

20 A fuller list (excluding Chinese and Indian Alchemy) would include Bolos of Mendes (c 2nd century BCE), Zosimos of Panopolis (c 3rd

century), Synesius (c 4th century), Morienus (c 7th century), Jabir ibn Hayyan (c 760-815), Al-Rhazi (866-925), Avicenna (980-1037), Al-Tughrai (1063-1120), Albertus Magnus (c 1200-1280), Roger Bacon (c 1220-1292), Arnald of Villanova (c 1235-1312), John Dee (1527-1608), Jean d'Espagnet (1564-1637), Michael Maier (1568-1622), Thomas Vaughan (1621-1666), Antoine-Joseph Pernety (1716-1801) and Mary Anne Atwood (1817-1910).

21 Titus Burckhardt, *Alchemy: Science of the Cosmos, Science of the Soul* (Shaftesbury: Element Books, 1986), 26.

22 Maurice Aniane, 'Notes on Alchemy the Cosmological "Yoga" of Medieval Christianity', *Material for Thought*, Spring 1976, http://www.giurfa.com/alchemy.html.

23 Julius Evola, *The Hermetic Tradition: Symbols & Teachings of the Royal Art* (Rochester, VT: Inner Traditions International, 1971), 27.

24 Faivre, *Access to Western Esotericism*, 168.

25 Burckhardt, *Alchemy*, 183.

26 Ibid., 189, emphasis mine.

27 Aniane, 'Notes on Alchemy.'

28 *The Six Keys of Eudoxus* (n.d.), first key, The Alchemy Web Site, http://www.alchemywebsite.com/eudoxus.html.

29 Marsilio Ficino, [1518?] *Book of the Chemical Art*, chap. 16, The Alchemy Web Site, http://www.alchemywebsite.com/ficino/html.

30 Aniane, 'Notes on Alchemy'.

31 *The Six Keys of Eudoxus*, fourth key.

32 Antoine Faivre recognizes seven stages of the Work. The Black stage = 1) Distillation; 2) Calcination; 3) Putrefaction; and 4) Solution-Dissolution. The White stage = 5) Coagulation; and 6) Vivification. The Red stage = 7), Multiplication or Projection (*Access to Western Esotericism*, 168-69).

33 d'Espagnet, *The Hermetic Arcanum*.

CHAPTER 5 – SPIRITUALITY AND COSMOLOGY

1 Quoted in Goodrick-Clarke, *Helena Blavatsky*, 197.

2 Bailey, *A Treatise on Cosmic Fire*, 829.

3 Heindel, *The Rosicrucian Cosmo-Conception*, 415.

4 Ellwood, *Theosophy*, 10.

5 Robert Ellwood, *Frodo's Quest: Living the Myth in The Lord of the Rings* (Wheaton, IL: Quest Books, 2002).

6 G de Purucker, *The Path of Compassion* (Pasadena, CA: Theosophical

University Press, 1986), section 2,
http://www.theosociety.org/pasadena/fso/ptcom-2.htm.

7   R Swinburne Clymer, *Compendium of Occult Laws* (Quakertown, PA:
    The Philosophical Publishing Company, 1966), chap. 2,
    http://www.geocities.com/collectumhermeticus/compendium.htm.

8   Ellwood, *Theosophy*, 25.

9   Besant, *The Ancient Wisdom*, 323.

10 Purucker, *The Path of Compassion*, section 2.

11 Niels Bronsted, 'Initiation', *The Journal of Esoteric Psychology*, Volume
    XII, Number 1, Spring/Summer 1998: 1-14.

12 J S Bakula, *Esoteric Psychology: A Model for the Development of
    Human Consciousness* (Seattle, WA: United Focus, 1978), 59.

13 See Rudolf Steiner, *Occult Science: An Outline* (London: Rudolf
    Steiner Press, 1979), 277.

14 Bronsted, 'Initiation'.

15 Swami Rajarshi Muni, *Yoga: The Ultimate Spiritual Path* (St. Paul,
    MN: Llewellyn Publications, 2001), 138.

16 Quoted in Robert K C Forman, 'What Does Mysticism Have to Teach
    Us About Consciousness?', *The Journal of Consciousness Studies*,
    Volume 5, Number 2, 1998.

17 Plotinus, [c250] *The First Ennead*, third tractate, Christian Classics
    Ethereal Library,
    http://www.ccel.org/ccel/plotinus/enneads.ii.iii.html.

18 Paul Brunton, *The Quest of the Overself* (London: Rider Books, 1996),
    314-15.

19 Boehme, *The Supersensual Life*, second dialogue.

CHAPTER 6 – THE FIRST INITIATION

1   Purucker, *The Path of Compassion*, section 2.

2   Brunton, *The Quest of the Overself*, 330.

3   Barbara Domalske, 'Three Essentials of Disciples', *The Beacon*,
    Volume LVIII, Number 2, March/April 1999.

4   Besant, *The Ancient Wisdom*, 330.

5   Rudolf Steiner, *How to Know Higher Worlds: A Modern Path of
    Initiation* (Great Barrington, MA: Anthroposophic Press, 1994), 139.

6   Besant, *The Ancient Wisdom*, 332.

7   Rudolf Steiner, *Esoteric Development: Selected Lectures and Writings*
    (Great Barrington, MA: SteinerBooks, 2003), 75.

8   Muni, *Yoga*, 86.

9   Steiner, *Occult Science*, 263.

10 Ibid., 295.

11 Alice A Bailey, *From Intellect to Intuition* (London and New York: Lucis Trust, 1987), 99.

12 Steiner, *Occult Science*, 235.

13 Dan Merkur, 'Stages of Ascension in Hermetic Rebirth', *Esoterica*, Volume 1, 1999, http://www.esoteric.msu.edu/merkur.html.

14 Steiner, *Occult Science*, 237.

15 Ibid.

16 Bailey, *Initiation, Human and Solar*, 114-15.

17 Ibid., 169.

18 Quoted in Dan Merkur, *Gnosis: An Esoteric Tradition of Mystical Visions and Unions* (Albany, NY: State University of New York Press, 1993), 59, emphasis mine.

19 Steiner, *How to Know Higher Worlds*, 143.

20 Forman, *Mysticism, Mind, Consciousness*, 13.

21 Quoted in Forman, 'What Does Mysticism'.

22 Ibid.

CHAPTER 7 – THE SECOND AND THIRD INITIATIONS

1   Bailey, *Initiation, Human and Solar*, 169.

2   Besant, *The Ancient Wisdom*, 337.

3   Zachary F Lansdowne, *The Rays and Esoteric Psychology* (York Beach, ME: Samuel Weiser, 1989), 35, emphasis mine.

4   Bakula, *Esoteric Psychology*, 61.

5   Steiner, *Occult Science*, 289.

6   Bailey, *The Rays and The Initiations*, 584.

7   Ibid., 578.

8   Bailey's *A Treatise on White Magic* (1934) is particularly concerned with helping to steer the first initiate through the 'astral waters'. This has a most definite relation to the work the first initiate undertakes (and must, if he is not to become trapped in his own fancies of spirituality). We can also speak of the Alchemist's 'Calcination' here: making consciousness 'dry', referring to the transcendence of the belief-investment plane, or, leaving religion behind.

9   Forman, 'What Does Mysticism'.

10 Mary Bailey, 'Esoteric Schools', *The Beacon*, Volume LVI, Number 8, March/April 1996, 13.

11 Forman, 'What Does Mysticism'.

12 *The Six Keys of Eudoxus*, second key.

13 Forman, 'What Does Mysticism'.

14 Steiner, *Occult Science*, 275.

15 Besant, *The Ancient Wisdom*, 78.

16 Bailey, *Initiation, Human and Solar*, 115.

17 Lansdowne, *The Rays and Esoteric Psychology*, 36.

18 Bronsted, 'Initiation'.

19 Quoted in Merkur, *Gnosis*, 59.

20 Vera Stanley Alder, *The Initiation of the World* (York Beach, ME: Samuel Weiser, 2000), 188, emphasis mine.

21 C W Leadbeater, [1925] *The Masters and the Path*, part III, chap. 9, Anand Gholap Theosophical Group, http://www.anandgholap.net/Masters_And_Path-CWL.htm.

22 Ibid.

23 Allan Combs, *The Radiance of Being*, 138.

24 Aniane, 'Notes on Alchemy'.

25 Ficino, *Book of the Chemical Art*, chap. 14, emphasis mine.

26 Halevi, *The Way of Kabbalah*, 187.

27 In his book *The Varieties of Religious Experience* (1902), William James also quotes Malwida von Meysenburg: 'I was alone upon the seashore as all these thoughts flowed over me, liberating and reconciling; and now again, as once before in distant days in the Alps of Dauphine, I was impelled to kneel down, this time before the illimitable ocean, symbol of the Infinite. I felt that I prayed as I had never prayed before, and knew now what prayer really is: to return from the solitude of individuation into the consciousness of unity with all that is, to kneel down as one that passes away, and to rise up as one imperishable. Earth, heaven, and sea resounded as in one vast world-encircling harmony. It was as if the chorus of all the great who had ever lived were about me. I felt myself one with them, and it appeared as if I heard their greeting: Thou too belongest to the company of those who overcome.' (lecture XVI and XVII, Council on Spiritual Practices, http://www.csp.org/experience/james-varieties/james-varieties16.html)

28 Forman, 'What Does Mysticism'.

29 Bailey, *Initiation, Human and Solar*, 117.

CHAPTER 8 – THE FOURTH AND FIFTH INITIATIONS

1 Kingsley, *Reality*, 102-03.

2 Purucker, *The Path of Compassion*, section 2.

3 Bailey, *Initiation, Human and Solar*, 89.

4 Jenny Wade, *Changes of Mind: A Holonomic Theory of the Evolution of Consciousness* (Albany, NY: State University of New York Press, 1996), 203.

5 Ibid., 204.

6 Bakula, *Esoteric Psychology*, 62-3.

7 Boehme, *The Supersensual Life*, second dialogue.

8 Burckhardt, *Alchemy*, 198.

9 Quoted in Joseph Campbell, *The Inner Reaches of Outer Space: Metaphor as Myth and as Religion* (New York: Harper & Row, 1986) 67.

10 Evelyn Underhill, [1911] *Mysticism: A Study in the Nature and Development of Spiritual Consciousness*, part 2, chap. 9, Christian Classics Ethereal Library, http://www.ccel.org/ccel/underhill/mysticism.iv.ix.html.

11 John Nash, *The Soul and Its Destiny* (Bloomington, IN: Authorhouse, 2004), 254.

12 Ibid., 255.

13 Steiner, *Occult Science*, 242.

14 Ibid.

15 Quoted in Merkur, *Gnosis*, 60.

16 Alder, *The Initiation of the World*, 80.

17 Purucker, *The Path of Compassion*, section 1, http://www.theosociety.org/pasadena/fso/ptcom-1.htm.

18 Ibid.

19 Besant, *The Ancient Wisdom*, 340.

20 Bailey, *A Treatise on Cosmic Fire*, 305.

21 Bailey, *Initiation, Human and Solar*, 90.

22 Leadbeater, *The Masters and the Path*, part I, chap. 1.

23 Purucker, *The Path of Compassion*, section 2.

24 Boehme, *The Supersensual Life*, second dialogue.

25 Bailey, *A Treatise on Cosmic Fire*, 121.

26 Bailey, *The Rays and The Initiations*, 660.

27 Besant, *The Ancient Wisdom*, 341-42.

28 Underhill, *Mysticism*, part 2, chap. 10,
   http://www.ccel.org/ccel/underhill/mysticism.iv.x.html.

29 Ibid.

CHAPTER 9 – THE HIGHER INITIATIONS

1 *The Six Keys of Eudoxus*, fifth key.

2 Aniane, 'Notes on Alchemy'.

3 Ficino, *Book of the Chemical Art*, chap. 15, emphasis mine.

4 Nash, *The Soul and Its Destiny*, 272.

5 Alder, *The Initiation of the World*, 80-81.

6 Muni, *Yoga*, 140.

7 Bailey, *A Treatise on Cosmic Fire*, 569.

8 Bailey, *Initiation, Human and Solar*, 106.

9 Ibid., 123, emphasis mine.

10 Ibid., 118.

11 Leadbeater, *The Masters and the Path*, part III, chap. 10.

12 Hall, *Lectures on Ancient Philosophy*, 334.

13 Leadbeater, *The Masters and the Path*, part III, chap. 15.

14 Bailey, *A Treatise on Cosmic Fire*, 697 and 121.

15 Bailey, *Initiation, Human and Solar*, 123.

16 Blavatsky, *The Secret Doctrine*, Vol. I, 573.

17 W T S Thackara, 'The Ancient Mysteries: A Great Light, A Force for
   Good', *Sunrise: Theosophical Perspectives*, November 1978,
   http://www.theosociety.org/pasadena/sunrise/28-78-9/oc-wtst.htm.

18 Agrippa, *De Occulta Philosophia*, book II, part 2, chap. LV,
   http://www.esotericarchives.com/agrippa/agripp2d.htm.

19 Purucker, *The Doctrine of the Spheres*, 44.

20 Purucker, *The Path of Compassion*, section 2.

21 Merkur, *Gnosis*, 61.

22 Halevi, *The Way of the Kabbalah*, 214.

23 Ibid.

24 Ibid., 216.

25 Ibid.

26 Purucker, *The Path of Compassion*, section 1, emphasis mine.

27 Eliphas Lévi, *The Key of the Mysteries* (London: Rider & Company,
   1977), 40, emphasis mine.

28 Bailey, *Initiation, Human and Solar*, 7-8, emphasis mine.

29 Bailey, *The Rays and The Initiations*, 697-98.

30 Ibid.

31 Ibid., 162.

32 Ibid.

33 *Poemandres, the Shepherd of Man*, in Mead, *Thrice Greatest Hermes*, http://www.gnosis.org/library/hermes1.html.

34 Ashlag, 'The Teachings of the Ten Sefirot'.

35 Purucker, *The Path of Compassion*, section 1.

CHAPTER 10 – CHANGING WORLDVIEWS

1 Hall, *Lectures on Ancient Philosophy*, 11.

2 Tarnas, *The Passion of the Western Mind*, 285.

3 For example Immanuel Kant (1724-1804), for whom what we see is what our reason – imposing its own order and organization on things – sees.

4 The constructivist view was popularized by Steven Katz, through his essay 'Language, Epistemology, and Mysticism' (in Steven T Katz, ed., *Mysticism and Philosophical Analysis*, New York: Oxford University Press, 1978, 22-74). There is no such thing as unmediated experience, so this view goes, but as Leon Schlamm points out in his essay 'Numinous Experience and Religious Language' (*Religious Studies*, Volume 28, Number 4, 1992, 533-551), Katz's view is an epistemological assumption, nothing more. There is no evidence, only conviction (based perhaps, suggests Schlamm, on the Wittgensteinian thesis, or else simply on personal self-reflection – see also note 15 below) that mystical experience is constituted by its religious tradition.

5 Besant, *The Ancient Wisdom*, 124.

6 David Loy, 'The Deconstruction of Buddhism', in Harold Coward and Toby Foshay, eds., with a conclusion by Jacques Derrida, *Derrida and Negative Theology* (Albany, NY: State University of New York Press, 1992), 250.

7 Tarnas, *The Passion of the Western Mind*, 353 and 404.

8 Huston Smith, *Why Religion Matters: The Fate of the Human Spirit in an Age of Reason* (New York: HarperCollins, 2001), 20-21.

9 J J Clarke, *Oriental Enlightenment: The Encounter Between Asian and Western Thought* (London and New York: Routledge, 1997), 211.

10 Daniel J Adams, 'Toward a Theological Understanding of Postmodernism', *Cross Currents*, Winter 1997-98, Volume 47, Issue 4,

http://www.crosscurrents.org/adams.htm.

11 Tarnas, *The Passion of the Western Mind*, 421.

12 Ibid., 346.

13 David Appelbaum and Jacob Needleman, eds., *Real Philosophy: An Anthology of the Universal Search for Meaning* (London: Arkana, 1990), 13.

14 Willis Harman, *Global Mind Change: The Promise of the 21st Century* (Sausalito, CA: Institute of Noetic Sciences / San Francisco: Berrett-Koehler Publishers, 1998), 127-28.

15 Two philosophers who denied the possibility of an experience of consciousness 'without an object' were David Hume (1711-1776) and G E Moore (1873-1958). Forman writes: 'Probably Hume and Moore tried to "catch" themselves without a perception on two or three quiet, furtive attempts. Furthermore, those attempts were no doubt part of their philosophical projects. Thus, probably without being aware of the experiential implications of their attitude of "trying to see something about consciousness", they could hardly have allowed their intellectual apparatus to "drop away" completely. Who is to say whether one of them might have achieved a silent consciousness after some years of meditation?' Our understanding of consciousness is, at root, grounded on empirical observations, and 'what is empirically possible for a human being is not something you, I, or Moore can decide *a priori*, with assertions based on what we *have* experienced so far' (*Mysticism, Mind, Consciousness*, 113-14).

CHAPTER 11 – SPIRITUAL PSYCHOLOGY I: CARL JUNG AND ROBERTO ASSAGIOLI

1 Abraham A Maslow, *Toward a Psychology of Being* (New York: Van Nostrand, 1968), 61.

2 John Welwood, ed., *The Meeting of the Ways: Explorations in East/West Psychology* (New York: Schocken, 1979) xi.

3 Clarke, *Oriental Enlightenment*, 150-51.

4 Douglas Russell, 'Psychosynthesis in Western Psychology', *Psychosynthesis Digest*, Volume 1, Number 1, Fall/Winter 1981, http://two.not2.org/psychosynthesis/articles/pd1-1.htm.

5 Dane Rudhyar, 'The Need for a Multi-level, Process-oriented Psychology', in Rosemarie Stewart, ed., *East Meets West: The Transpersonal Approach* (Wheaton, IL: The Theosophical Publishing House, 1981), 136-45.

6 Bakula, *Esoteric Psychology*, 58.

7 Francis Vaughan and Roger Walsh, eds., *Path Beyond Ego: The*

Transpersonal Vision (Los Angeles: Jeremy P Tarcher/Putnam, 1993), 34.

8   Michael Daniels, *Shadow, Self, Spirit: Essays in Transpersonal Psychology* (Exeter: Imprint Academic, 2005), 13.

9   Carl Jung, *Archetypes and the Collective Unconscious* (Princeton, NJ: Princeton University Press, 1969), 58.

10 William Bloom, ed., *Holistic Revolution: The Essential New Age Reader* (London: Allen Lane/The Penguin Press, 2000), 51.

11 Carl Jung, *Modern Man in Search of a Soul* (London: Routledge, 2003), 211.

12 See Gerhard Wehr, 'C G Jung in the Context of Christian Esotericism and Cultural History', in *Modern Esoteric Spirituality*, 381-99.

13 Hoeller, *Gnosticism*, 171.

14 Quoted in Quinn, *The Only Tradition*, 272.

15 Quoted in Gerhard Wehr, *Jung: A Biography* (London: Shambhala, 2001), 203.

16 Carl Jung, *Psychology and the East* (London: Routledge and Kegan Paul, 1978), 157.

17 Quoted in Robert Ellwood, *The Politics of Myth: A Study of C. G. Jung, Mircea Eliade, and Joseph Campbell* (Albany, NY: State University of New York Press, 1999), 70.

18 Bakula, *Esoteric Psychology*, 57.

19 Carl Jung, *Mysterium Coniunctionis: An Inquiry Into the Separation and Synthesis of Psychic Opposites in Alchemy* (Princeton, NJ: Princeton University Press, 1963), 189.

20 Quoted in Wouter J Hanegraaff, *New Age Religion and Western Culture: Esotericism in the Mirror of Secular Thought* (Leiden: E J Brill, 1996), 503, emphasis mine. This is taken from his poetic work *The Seven Sermons to the Dead* (c1916), ascribed to the Gnostic Basilides.

21 Not to be confused with Ken Wilber's 'all quadrants, all levels' (AQAL) model.

22 Quoted in Smith, *The World's Religions*, 19.

23 Douglas Russell, 'Seven Basic Constructs of Psychosynthesis', *Psychosynthesis Digest*, Volume 1, Number 2, Spring/Summer 1982, http://www.two.not2.org/psychosynthesis/articles/pd1-2.htm.

24 Roberto Assagioli, *Psychosynthesis: The Definitive Guide to the Principles and Techniques of Psychosynthesis* (London: Thorsons, 1993), 17.

25 Ibid., 17-18.

26 Ibid., 18.

27 John Welwood, *Toward a Psychology of Awakening: Buddhism, Psychotherapy, and the Path of Personal and Spiritual Transformation* (London: Shambhala, 2000), 207-13.

CHAPTER 12 – SPIRITUAL PSYCHOLOGY II: KEN WILBER

1 Frank Visser, 'Post-Metaphysics and Beyond: The AQAL Framework as Kosmic Compass', 2003, http://www.integralworld.net.

2 Robert P Turner, 'Esoteric Psychology: Expanding Transpersonal Vision', *The Journal of Esoteric Psychology*, Volume IX, Number 1, 1995, 90-102.

3 Ibid.

4 And by extending the end point of consciousness evolution to cosmic realms, 'it de-emphasizes any future-oriented longing for personal liberation and promotes the never-ending opportunity for service in the present. And finally, it links the individual to the cosmos, providing a context within which to fulfil his or her unique, destined role not only within the planetary Whole but within the cosmic Whole as well.' (ibid.)

5 Named after the Gnostic Pleroma, it is certainly a 'fullness' of some kind. If the Atman experience is of some Whole looking out from behind oneself's eyes at Itself, here there is no 'oneself' really, and we are not talking about an all-levels Whole either. The subject is matter, the object is matter – if we are still entitled to use the terms 'subject' and 'object' here that is. If there *was* just the one level of existence – matter – then the Atman experience would simply be the first initiation experience. If we are aware of the physical consciousness 'light', then we are aware that the apparently objective world and self are just 'born' on this light.

6 The Archaic is somewhat of a transitional stage between the Pleromatic and the Magic.

7 There is no ordinary intelligent appreciation of the self and the world here. Thus the world for the child *is*, and the world for our prehistoric ancestors *was*, a truly 'magical' place, where one object could be made to stand for another. (In the case of a child, a doll for a cartoon character, say – which of course advertisers cash in on.) In this stage also, the *Mother* (the child's mother/Earth Mother) is/was somewhat of a revered deity.

8 Definite individual selfhood is/was not quite here yet. The 'I' tends/tended to be 'attached' to something else. When the mature or ideal-type adult says 'I', he *means* 'I', pure and simple. When the youth says 'I' though, there tends to be more of a qualification e.g. I *as an*

American, or I *as a Muslim*. *Language* skills are/were developed at this stage, says Wilber, and whilst Mental man sees a universe of hard materiality, with an existence that might be completely by accident and meaningless, the youth tends to (and Mythic man did) hold on to a *Myth* of some kind. He possesses/possessed *religiosity*. This is why, as Assagioli pointed out, youths are more prone to such things as racism and fervent nationalism – also, an *irrational* mysticism.

9   Gebser called this the *perspectival* worldview (the 'me here, world there' sense). The mental structure *operates* to fix the location of the ego in objective space, resulting in rigidity and a self-centred inability to go beyond its own narrow confines. Said Gebser: 'Compelled to emphasize his ego ever more strongly because of (its) isolating fixity, man faces the world in hostile confrontation. The world in turn reinforces this confrontation by taking on an ever-expanding spatial volume (as in the discovery of America) or extent, which the growing strength of the ego attempts to conquer' (quoted in Combs, *The Radiance of Being*, 111).

10   The adult is aware of an objective physical realm – the 'cold hard reality' presented by materialistic science. The child is not (this is why magic exists to him); and the adolescent, though he may have grown out of belief in Santa Claus, is still not quite ready to see America (if he was an American) as just another nation, and life as mechanical and meaningless. In our universities we have people with highly developed Mental consciousnesses, but we also have people whose dominating consciousness is Centauric. 'Centaurs' do not see what materialistic science sees, but neither do they see what individuals at the Low Subtle stage of evolution see (or would see) either. The world for them is neither material nor spiritual, but reality is in the mind of the beholder. The point to remember about all these stages, says Wilber, is that each new stage brings with it a new perspective, and a new 'psychic house', but the previous stages are still there under the surface, and can and do pop up again at times – which can be for good or for bad.

11   Ken Wilber, *A Theory of Everything: An Integral Vision for Business, Politics, Science and Spirituality* (Dublin: Gateway, 2001), 12.

12   Ken Wilber, *Integral Psychology: Consciousness, Spirit, Psychology, Therapy* (Boston and London: Shambhala, 2000), 109.

13   Ken Wilber, *The Atman Project: A Transpersonal View of Human Development* (Wheaton, IL: Quest Books, 1996), 71.

14   Ibid., 70.

15   Ibid., 171-72.

16   Ibid., 77.

17 In this connection, we might consider Gebser's final *Integral* stage/structure, where human beings experience the world through their *consciousnesses*, and as such have an awareness of themselves as continually becoming, rather than discontinuously being. The Integral structure/stage reveals itself in the *aperspectival* worldview, which places the ego back into the world, as the world no longer has an objective status. Gebser saw evidence for an emerging Integral stage/structure in the 'discoveries' of the new quantum physicists (as well as in some types of modern art), and Allan Combs believes that an aperspectival worldview will dominate 21st century civilization.

18 Wilber, *The Atman Project*, 173.

19 Ibid., 79.

20 Quoted in Wilber, ibid.

21 Ibid.

22 Ibid., 81.

23 Ibid., 83.

24 But the individual has to get over himself as the soul, remember. Hence the Dark Night of the Soul/Crucifixion/Renunication stage.

25 Ibid., 84.

26 In the system of Sri Aurobindo, the *Overmind* consciousness would equate to the buddhic consciousness. This 'mindset' fully belongs to the fourth initiate. Above/beyond this, the *Supermind* fully belongs to the Adept, and below the Overmind (and evolutionarily before it) is the *Intuitive Mind* (third initiate), *Illumined Mind* (second initiate), and *Higher Mind* (first initiate). Like Muni and esotericists generally, Aurobindo recognizes that evolution doesn't (or needn't) stop at the Supermind level – there is an ultimate God or *Saccidananda* consciousness (cf. seventh initiation). Nevertheless, the Supermind is a major staging post: the point at which Man, who has been travelling from Nature to Supernature, becomes Superman.

27 Ibid., 86.

28 Ibid., 85.

29 Ibid.

30 Besant, *The Ancient Wisdom*, 330.

31 Wilber, *The Atman Project*, 86.

CHAPTER 13 – CHALLENGES OF THE ESOTERIC VIEW

1 Schuon, *The Transcendent Unity of Religions*, 48.

2 Faivre, *Access to Western Esotericism*, 296.

3 Heindel, *The Rosicrucian Cosmo-Conception*, 435-36.

4   Quoted in Nicolescu, *Science, Meaning, & Evolution*, 129.

5   Burckhardt, *Alchemy*, 51, emphasis mine.

6   Schuon, *Light on the Ancient Worlds*, 111, emphasis mine.

7   Faivre, *Access to Western Esotericism*, 292.

8   Steiner, *Esoteric Development*, 90.

9   Purucker, *The Esoteric Tradition*, chap. 6.

10   Hall, *Lectures on Ancient Philosophy*, 32.

11   *Poemandres, the Shepherd of Man*.

Bibliography

Adams, Daniel J. 'Toward a Theological Understanding of Postmodernism.' *Cross Currents*, Winter 1997-98, Volume 47, Issue 4. First appeared in *Metanoia*, Spring/Summer 1997. Available online at http://www.crosscurrents.org/adams.htm.

Agrippa, Heinrich Cornelius. [1510] *De Occulta Philosophia*. Digital edition by Joseph H Peterson, 2000. Available online at http://www.esotericarchives.com.

Alder, Vera Stanley. *The Initiation of the World*. York Beach, ME: Samuel Weiser, 2000. First published 1968 by Lucis Trust.

Aniane, Maurice. 'Notes on Alchemy the Cosmological "Yoga" of Medieval Christianity'. *Material for Thought*, Spring 1976. Available online at http://www.giurfa.com/alchemy.html.

Appelbaum, David, and Jacob Needleman. *Real Philosophy: An Anthology of the Universal Search for Meaning*. London: Arkana, 1990.

Ashlag, Rabbi Y. 'The Teachings of the Ten Sefirot'. Bnei Baruch World Center for Kabbalah Studies, 1996. Available online at http://www.kabbalah.info/engkab/commentary.htm.

Assagioli, Roberto. *Psychosynthesis: The Definitive Guide to the Principles and Techniques of Psychosynthesis*. London: Thorsons, 1993. First published 1965.

Bailey, Alice A. *From Intellect to Intuition*. 5th ed. London and New York: Lucis Trust, 1987. First published 1932.

Initiation, Human and Solar. 6th ed. London and New York: Lucis Trust, 1992. First published 1922.

The Light of the Soul: A Paraphrase of The Yoga Sutras of Patanjali. 5th ed. London and New York: Lucis Trust, 1989. First published 1927.

The Rays and The Initiations. Vol. V, *A Treatise on the Seven Rays*. 5th ed. London and New York: Lucis Trust, 1993. First published 1960.

A Treatise on Cosmic Fire. 4th ed. London and New York: Lucis Trust, 1989. First published 1925.

A Treatise on White Magic or The Way of The Disciple. 6th ed. London and New York: Lucis Trust, 1991. First published 1934.

Bailey, Mary. 'Esoteric Schools.' *The Beacon*, Volume LVI, Number 8, March/April 1996: 12-16.

Bakula, J S. *Esoteric Psychology: A Model for the Development of Human Consciousness*. Seattle, WA: United Focus, 1978.

Besant, Annie. [1897] *The Ancient Wisdom: An Outline of Theosophical Teachings*. 14th reprint. Adyar, Madras: The Theosophical Publishing House, 1997.

Blavatsky, H P. [1888] *The Secret Doctrine: The Synthesis of Science, Religion, and Philosophy*. 2 vols. Centennial ed. Pasadena, CA: Theosophical University Press, 1988.

Bloom, William, ed. *Holistic Revolution: The Essential New Age Reader*. London: Allen Lane/The Penguin Press, 2000.

Boehme, Jacob. [1622] *Of Regeneration, or the New Birth*. Christian Classics Ethereal Library. Available online at http://www.ccel.org/b/boehme/way/regeneration.html.

[1622] *The Supersensual Life, or The Life Which is Above Sense*. Christian Classics Ethereal Library. Available online at http://www.ccel.org/b/boehme/way/supersensual_life.html.

Borella, Jean. 'René Guénon and the Traditionalist School.' In *Modern Esoteric Spirituality*, edited by Antoine Faivre and Jacob Needleman, 330-58. London: SCM Press Ltd, 1993. First published 1992 by The Crossroad Publishing Company.

Broek, Roelof van den, and Wouter J Hanegraaff, eds. *Gnosis and Hermeticism from Antiquity to Modern Times*. Albany, NY: State University of New York Press, 1998.

Brons, David. 'The Valentinian View of the Creation.' 2003. Available online at
http://www.gnosis.org/library/valentinus/Valentinian_Creation.htm.

Bronsted, Niels. 'Initiation.' *The Journal of Esoteric Psychology*, Volume XII, Number 1, Spring/Summer 1998: 1-14.

Brunton, Paul. *The Quest of the Overself*. London: Rider Books, 1996. First published 1937.

Burckhardt, Titus. *Alchemy: Science of the Cosmos, Science of the Soul*. Translated by William Stoddart. Shaftesbury: Element Books, 1986. First published 1967 by Stuart and Watkins.

Campbell, Joseph. *The Inner Reaches of Outer Space: Metaphor as Myth and as Religion*. New York: Harper & Row, 1986.

Clarke, J J. *Oriental Enlightenment: The Encounter Between Asian and Western Thought*. London and New York: Routledge, 1997.

Clymer, R Swinburne. *Compendium of Occult Laws*. Quakertown, PA: The Philosophical Publishing Company, 1966. Also available online at http://www.geocities.com/collectumhermeticus/compendium.htm.

Combs, Allan. *The Radiance of Being: Complexity, Chaos and the Evolution of Consciousness*. St Paul, MN: Paragon House, 1996. First published 1995 by Floris Books.

Coomaraswamy, Ananda K. *Selected Papers: Metaphysics*. Edited by Roger Lipsey. Bollingen Series 89. Princeton, NJ: Princeton University Press, 1977.

Coward, Harold, and Toby Foshay, eds., with a conclusion by Jacques Derrida. *Derrida and Negative Theology*. Albany, NY: State University of New York Press, 1992.

Cutsinger, James S. 'An Open Letter on Tradition'. 2001. First appeared in *Modern Age*, 36:3, 1994. Available online at http://www.cutsinger.net/pdf/letter.pdf.

Daniels, Michael. *Shadow, Self, Spirit: Essays in Transpersonal Psychology*. Exeter: Imprint Academic, 2005.

d'Espagnet, Jean. [1623] *The Hermetic Arcanum*. The Alchemy Web Site. Available online at http://www.alchemywebsite.com/harcanum.html.

Dilworth, David A. *Philosophy in World Perspective: A Comparative Hermeneutic of the Major Theories*. New Haven and London: Yale University Press, 1989.

Domalske, Barbara. 'Three Essentials of Disciples.' *The Beacon*, Volume LVIII, Number 2, March/April 1999: 21-23.

Ellwood, Robert. *Frodo's Quest: Living the Myth in The Lord of the Rings*. Wheaton, IL: Quest Books, 2002.

The Politics of Myth: A Study of C. G. Jung, Mircea Eliade, and Joseph Campbell. Albany, NY: State University of New York Press, 1999.

Theosophy: A Modern Expression of the Wisdom of the Ages. 2nd printing. Wheaton, IL: Quest Books, 1994.

Evola, Julius. *The Hermetic Tradition: Symbols & Teachings of the Royal Art*. Translated by E E Rehmus. Rochester, VT: Inner Traditions International, 1971. First published 1931 by Laterza.

'On the Secret of Degeneration.' *Deutsches Volkstum*, Number 11, 1938. Available online at http://pages.zoom.co.uk/thuban/html/evola.html.

Faivre, Antoine. *Access to Western Esotericism*. Albany, NY: State University of New York Press, 1994.

'Ancient and Medieval Sources of Modern Esoteric Movements.' In *Modern Esoteric Spirituality*, edited by Antoine Faivre and Jacob Needleman, 1-70. London: SCM Press Ltd, 1993. First published 1992 by The Crossroad Publishing Company.

Theosophy, Imagination, Tradition: Studies in Western Esotericism. Translated by Christine Rhone. Albany, NY: State University of New York Press, 2000. First published 1996 as *Accès de l'ésotérisme occidental, Tome II* by Editions Gallimard.

Faivre, Antoine, and Wouter J Hanegraaff, eds. *Western Esotericism and the Science of Religion.* Leuven: Peeters, 1998.

Faivre, Antoine, and Jacob Needleman, eds. *Modern Esoteric Spirituality.* London: SCM Press Ltd, 1993. First published 1992 by The Crossroad Publishing Company.

Fernando, Ranjit, ed. *The Unanimous Tradition: Essays on the Essential Unity of All Religions.* 2nd ed. Colombo: The Sri Lanka Institute of Traditional Studies, 1999.

Ficino, Marsilio. [1518?] *Book of the Chemical Art.* The Alchemy Web Site. Available online at http://www.alchemywebsite.com/ficino.html.

Forman, Robert K C. *Mysticism, Mind, Consciousness.* Albany, NY: State University of New York Press, 1999.

'What Does Mysticism Have to Teach Us About Consciousness?' *The Journal of Consciousness Studies*, Volume 5, Number 2, 1998: 185-201.

Godwin, Joscelyn. *The Theosophical Enlightenment.* Albany, NY: State University of New York Press, 1994.

Goodrick-Clarke, Nicholas, ed. *Helena Blavatsky.* Berkeley, CA: North Atlantic Books, 2004.

Guénon, René. *The Reign of Quantity and The Signs of the Times.* Translated by Lord Northbourne. London: Luzac & Company, 1953. First published 1945 by Editions Gallimard.

Halevi, Z'ev ben Shimon. *The Way of Kabbalah.* Boston, MA: Weiser, 1976.

Hall, Manly P. *Journey in Truth.* Los Angeles: Philosophical Research Society, 1945.

Lectures on Ancient Philosophy: An Introduction to Practical Ideals. Rev. ed. Los Angeles: Philosophical Research Society, 1984. First published 1929.

The Wisdom of the Knowing Ones. Gnosticism: The Key to Esoteric Christianity. Los Angeles: Philosophical Research Society, 2000.

Hanegraaff, Wouter J. 'On the Construction of "Esoteric Traditions"'. In *Western Esotericism and the Science of Religion*, edited by Antoine Faivre and Wouter J Hanegraaff, 11-61. Leuven: Peeters, 1998.

New Age Religion and Western Culture: Esotericism in the Mirror of Secular Thought. Leiden: E. J. Brill, 1996.

'Some Remarks on the Study of Western Esotericism.' *Esoterica*, Volume 1, 1999: 3-19. Also available online at http://www.esoteric.msu.edu/hanegraaff.html.

Hanegraaff, Wouter J. ed., in collaboration with Antoine Faivre, Roelof van den Broek, and Jean-Pierre Brach. *Dictionary of Gnosis and Western Esotericism.* Leiden: E J Brill, 2005.

Harman, Willis. *Global Mind Change: The Promise of the 21st Century.* 2nd ed. Sausalito, CA: Institute of Noetic Sciences / San Francisco: Berrett-Koehler Publishers, 1998.

Hartmann, Franz. [1887] *The Life of Paracelsus and the Substance of his Teachings.* San Diego: Wizards Bookshelf, 1985.

Heindel, Max. *The Rosicrucian Cosmo-Conception or Mystic Christianity.* 3rd ed. Oceanside, CA: The Rosicrucian Fellowship, 1992. First published 1909.

Hoeller, Stephan A. *Gnosticism: New Light on the Ancient Tradition of Inner Knowing.* Wheaton, IL: Quest Books, 2002.

Huxley, Aldous. *The Perennial Philosophy.* New York: Harper & Row, 1990. First published 1944.

James, William. [1902] *The Varieties of Religious Experience.* The Council on Spiritual Practices. Available online at http://www.csp.org/experience/james-varieties/james-varieties.html.

Julian the Apostate (Flavius Claudius Julianus). [c351] *Oration upon the Sovereign Sun. Addressed to Sallust.* Online edition by Roger Pearse, 2003. Available at http://www.tertullian.org/fathers/julian_apostate_1_sun.htm.

Jung, Carl G. *Archetypes and the Collective Unconscious.* Princeton, NJ: Princeton University Press, 1969.

Modern Man in Search of a Soul. London: Routledge, 2003. First published 1933.

Mysterium Coniunctionis: An Inquiry Into the Separation and Synthesis of Psychic Opposites in Alchemy. Princeton, NJ: Princeton University Press, 1963.

Psychology and the East. London: Routledge and Kegan Paul, 1978.

[1916?] *The Seven Sermons to the Dead written by Basilides in Alexandria, the City where the East toucheth the West.* The Gnostic Society Library. Available online at http://www.gnosis.org/library/7Sermons.htm.

Katz, Steven. 'Language, Epistemology, and Mysticism'. In *Mysticism and Philosophical Analysis*, edited by Steven T Katz, 22-74. New York: Oxford University Press, 1978.

Kingsley, Peter. *Reality*. Inverness, CA: The Golden Sufi Center Publishing, 2003.

Lansdowne, Zachary F. *The Rays and Esoteric Psychology*. York Beach, ME: Samuel Weiser, 1989.

Leadbeater, C W. [1925] *The Masters and the Path*. Anand Gholap Theosophical Group. Available online at http://www.anandgholap.net/Masters_And_Path-CWL.htm. First published by the Theosophical Publishing House.

Lévi, Eliphas. [1861] *The Key of the Mysteries*. Translated by Aleister Crowley. London: Rider & Company, 1977. First published 1913.

Loy, David. 'The Deconstruction of Buddhism.' In *Derrida and Negative Theology*, edited by Harold Coward and Toby Foshay with a conclusion by Jacques Derrida, 227-53. Albany, NY: State University of New York Press, 1992.

Nonduality: A Study in Comparative Philosophy. Atlantic Highlands, NJ: Humanities Press International, 1997. First published 1988.

Macchio, Joseph P. *The Orthodox Suppression of Original Christianity*. 2003. Available online at www.essenes.net/conspireindex.html.

Maslow, Abraham A. *Toward a Psychology of Being*. 2nd ed. New York: Van Nostrand, 1968. First published 1962.

Mead, G R S. [1906] *Thrice Greatest Hermes: Studies in Hellenistic Theosophy and Gnosis*. The Gnostic Society Library. Available online at http://www.gnosis.org/library/hermet.htm.

Merkur, Dan. *Gnosis: An Esoteric Tradition of Mystical Visions and Unions*. Albany, NY: State University of New York Press, 1993.

'Stages of Ascension in Hermetic Rebirth.' *Esoterica*, Volume 1, 1999: 79-96. Also available online at http://www.esoteric.msu.edu/merkur.html.

Mitchell, Brett. *The Sun is Alive: The Spirit, Consciousness, and Intelligence of our Solar System*. Carlsbad, CA: Esoteric Publishing, 1997.

Muni, Swami Rajarshi. *Yoga: The Ultimate Spiritual Path*. St Paul, MN: Llewellyn Publications, 2001.

Nash, John. *The Soul and Its Destiny*. Bloomington, IN: Authorhouse, 2004.

Needleman, Jacob. 'Introduction II'. In *Modern Esoteric Spirituality*, edited by Antoine Faivre and Jacob Needleman, xxiii-xxx. London: SCM Press Ltd, 1993. First published 1992 by The Crossroad Publishing Company.

Nicolescu, Basarab. *Science, Meaning, & Evolution: The Cosmology of Jacob Boehme*. Translated by Rob Baker. New York: Parabola Books, 1991. First published 1988 as *La Science, le sens, et l'évolution: Essai sur Jakob Boehme* by Editions du Félin.

Pernety, Antoine-Joseph. [1758?] *A Treatise on The Great Art: A System of Physics According to Hermetic Philosophy and Theory and Practice of the Magisterium*. E-book edition by Flaming Sword Productions, 1997. Available online at http://www.hermetics.org/pdf/alchemy/The_Great_Art.pdf.

Perry, Whitall N. 'The Revival of Interest in Tradition'. In *The Unanimous Tradition: Essays on the Essential Unity of All Religions*, edited by Ranjit Fernando, 3-16. 2nd ed. Colombo: The Sri Lanka Institute of Traditional Studies, 1999.

Plotinus. [c250] *The Six Enneads*. Translated by Stephen MacKenna and B S Page. Christian Classics Ethereal Library. Available online at http://www.ccel.org/ccel/plotinus/enneads.html.

Prem, Sri Krishna. *The Yoga of the Bhagavat Gita*. London: John Watkins, 1958.

Purucker, G de. *The Doctrine of the Spheres*. Vol. VII, *Esoteric Teachings*. San Diego, CA: Point Loma Publications, 1987.

The Esoteric Tradition. Pasadena, CA: Theosophical University Press, 1940. Available online at http://www.theosociety.org/pasadena/et/et-hp.htm.

The Path of Compassion. Pasedena, CA: Theosophical University Press, 1986. Available online at http://www.theosociety.org/pasadena/fso/ptcom-hp.htm.

Quinn, William W, Jr. *The Only Tradition*. Albany, NY: State University of New York Press, 1997.

Quispel, Gilles. 'The Asclepius: From the Hermetic Lodge in Alexandria to the Greek Eucharist and the Roman Mass.' In *Gnosis and Hermeticism from Antiquity to Modern Times*, edited by Roelof van den Broek and Wouter J Hanegraaff, 69-77. Albany: NY: State University of New York Press, 1998.

Riffard, Pierre A. 'The Esoteric Method'. In *Western Esotericism and the Science of Religion*, edited by Antoine Faivre and Wouter J Hanegraaff, 63-74. Leuven: Peeters, 1998.

Rudhyar, Dane. 'The Need for a Multi-level, Process-oriented Psychology'. In *East Meets West: The Transpersonal Approach*, edited by Rosemarie Stewart, 136-45. Wheaton, IL: The Theosophical Publishing House, 1981.

Russell, Douglas. 'Psychosynthesis in Western Psychology.' *Psychosynthesis Digest*, Volume 1, Number 1, Fall/Winter 1981. Available online at http://two.not2.org/psychosynthesis/articles/pd1-1.htm.

'Seven Basic Constructs of Psychosynthesis.' *Psychosynthesis Digest*, Volume 1, Number 2, Spring/Summer 1982. Available online at http://two.not2.org/psychosynthesis/articles/pd1-2.htm.

Schaya, Leo. 'Some Universal Aspects of Judaism'. In *The Unanimous Tradition: Essays on the Essential Unity of All Religions*, edited by Ranjit Fernando, 57-75. 2nd ed. Colombo: The Sri Lanka Institute of Traditional Studies, 1999.

Schlamm, Leon. 'Numinous Experience and Religious Language'. *Religious Studies: An International Journal for the Philosophy of Religion*, Volume 28, Number 4, 1992: 553-551.

Scholem, Gershom. *Major Trends in Jewish Mysticism*. 3rd ed. New York: Schocken, 1961.

Schuon, Frithjof. *Light on the Ancient Worlds*. Bloomington, IN: World Wisdom Books, 1984. First published 1965 by Perennial Books.

'Sophia Perennis and the Theory of Evolution and Progress.' 2001. Available online at http://www.frithjof-schuon.com/evolution-engl.htm.

The Transcendent Unity of Religions. 2nd ed. Wheaton, IL: Quest Books, 1993. First published 1957.

Sherrard, Philip. 'How Do I See the Universe and Man's Place in It?' Paper presented at the conference on Modern Science and Traditional Religions Consultation, Windsor, England, March 1976. Available online at http://www.incommunion.org/articles/older-issues/the-universe-and-mans-place-in-it.

Smith, Huston. *Beyond the Postmodern Mind*. 4th printing. Wheaton, IL: Quest Books, 1996.

Why Religion Matters: The Fate of the Human Spirit in an Age of Disbelief. New York: HarperCollins, 2001.

The World's Religions: Our Great Wisdom Traditions. Rev. ed. New York: HarperCollins, 1991. First published 1958.

Steiner, Rudolf. *Esoteric Development: Selected Lectures and Writings*. Great Barrington, MA: SteinerBooks, 2003.

How to Know Higher Worlds: A Modern Path of Initiation. Translated by Christopher Bamford. Great Barrington, MA: Anthroposophic Press, 1994. First published 1961 by Rudolf Steiner Verlag.

Occult Science: An Outline. Translated by George and Mary Adams. 2nd reprint. London: Rudolf Steiner Press, 1979. First published 1910.

Stewart, Rosemarie, ed. *East Meets West: The Transpersonal Approach*. Wheaton, IL: The Theosophical Publishing House, 1981.

Stuckrad, Kocku von. *Western Esotericism: A Brief History of Secret Knowledge*. Translated by Nicholas Goodrick-Clarke. London and Oakville, CT: Equinox Publishing Ltd, 2005.

Tarnas, Richard. *The Passion of the Western Mind: Understanding the Ideas That Have Shaped Our World View*. London: Pimlico, 1996. First published 1991 by Crown.

Thackara, W T S. 'The Ancient Mysteries: A Great Light, A Force for Good'. *Sunrise: Theosophical Perspectives*, November 1978. Available online at http://www.theosociety.org/pasadena/sunrise/28-78-9/oc-wtst.htm.

'The Perennial Philosophy'. *Sunrise: Theosophical Perspectives*, April/May 1984. Available online at http://www.theosociety.org/pasadena/sunrise/33-83-4/ge-wtst.htm.

Turner, Robert P. 'Esoteric Psychology: Expanding Transpersonal Vision'. *The Journal of Esoteric Psychology*, Volume IX, Number 1, 1995: 90-102.

Underhill, Evelyn. [1911] *Mysticism: A Study in the Nature and Development of Spiritual Consciousness*. Christian Classics Ethereal Library. Available online at http://www.ccel.org/ccel/underhill/mysticism.html.

Versluis, Arthur. 'Mysticism, and the Study of Esotericism: Methods in the Study of Esotericism, Part II'. *Esoterica*, Volume 5, 2003: 27-40. Also available online at http://www.esoteric.msu.edu/volumev/mysticism.htm.

Wisdom's Children: A Christian Esoteric Tradition. Albany, NY: State University of New York Press, 1999.

Vaughan, Francis, and Roger Walsh, eds. *Path Beyond Ego: The Transpersonal Vision*. Los Angeles: Jeremy P Tarcher/Putnam, 1993.

Visser, Frank. 'Post-Metaphysics and Beyond: The AQAL Framework as Kosmic Compass'. 2003. Available online at http://www.integralworld.net.

Wade, Jenny. *Changes of Mind: A Holonomic Theory of the Evolution of Consciousness*. Albany, NY: State University of New York Press, 1996.

Wehr, Gerhard. 'C. G. Jung in the Context of Christian Esotericism and Cultural History'. In *Modern Esoteric Spirituality*, edited by Antoine Faivre and Jacob Needleman, 381-99. London: SCM Press Ltd, 1993. First published 1992 by The Crossroad Publishing Company.

Jung: A Biography. London: Shambhala, 2001.

Welwood, John, ed. *The Meeting of the Ways: Explorations in East/West Psychology*. New York: Schocken, 1979.

Toward a Psychology of Awakening: Buddhism, Psychotherapy, and the Path of Personal and Spiritual Transformation. London: Shambhala, 2000.

Wilber, Ken. *The Atman Project: A Transpersonal View of Human Development*. New ed. Wheaton, IL: Quest Books, 1996.

Integral Psychology: Consciousness, Spirit, Psychology, Therapy. Boston and London: Shambhala, 2000.

A Theory of Everything: An Integral Vision for Business, Politics, Science and Spirituality. Dublin: Gateway, 2001.

Yates, Frances A. *Giordano Bruno and the Hermetic Tradition*. New York: Random House, 1969. First published 1964 by Routledge and Kegan Paul.

Index

Alder -
Assagio
Hoeller